WOOD ON THE BOTTOM

GREAT LAKES SHIPWRECKS

FREDERICK STONEHOUSE

Avery Color Studios, Inc.
Gwinn, Michigan

© 2009 Avery Color Studios, Inc.

ISBN-13: 978-1-892384-50-8
ISBN-10: 1-892384-50-7

Library of Congress Control Number: 2009922379

First Edition–2009

10 9 8 7 6 5 4 3 2 1

Published by Avery Color Studios, Inc.
Gwinn, Michigan 49841

Cover photos: Author's Collection

✳ TABLE OF CONTENTS ✳

✳ INTRODUCTION ✳

A few years ago I wrote a book called *Steel on the Bottom* (Avery Color Studios, 2006), a close look at a dozen or so Great Lakes steel shipwrecks that especially interest me. Readers liked the book as judged by sales and very positive comments.

When I considered my next project it was logical to extrapolate the concept to *Wood on the Bottom* and thus this book was born. Again there wasn't any particular logic to the shipwrecks I selected beyond the fact they interest me more than others. In the case of the *Rouse Simmons* I thought it was a good opportunity to present a different view of the wreck than the treacle approach so common today. I realize I will be pummeled for my conclusions on the true story of the wreck but regardless it is a tale worth telling with a more straightforward slant.

Whether the book is successful or not is, as always, up to the reader. *Enjoy.*

✳ 1

SANDUSKY

Typical Of The Breed

The big *Sandusky* is another of the sailing grain carriers that met her end on the stormy lakes. While her working career was very typical of the breed, it was the discovery of her wreckage 125 years after the loss that was unique. But let's start at the beginning.

She was built in Sandusky, Ohio in 1848 and measured 110-feet by 25.5 feet and 225 gross tons (old measure). As befit her small size, she only had two masts. The foremast was square rigged and the mainmast fore and aft thus she was technically a brig (also called a "brigantine"). Brigs were common in the early days of Great Lakes sailing but by the 1860s had largely disappeared. Schooners (fore and after rigged on all masts) were much easier to handle and took fewer and less trained crew. This meant they were cheaper to operate, always an important consideration.

Following her fitting out she went directly into the grain trade from Chicago to Buffalo, backhauling general freight. She was reasonably fast, once making the trip in seven days, a very quick run in an age when speed counted at least for the first load of the season. She could carry about 10,000 bushels of grain.

She had a few problems as she earned her way across the lakes. The same year she was launched she fetched ashore on Long Point on the Canadian side of Lake Erie. It was a dangerous ship trap and she was lucky to have been hauled off without major damage. In 1851 she sprang a leak serious enough to cause her to return to port for repairs. Later in the year she found bottom on a shoal in western Lake Erie and had to dump some of her cargo to come free. In June, 1855, she went ashore on Beaver Island in northern Lake Michigan. Again, dumping cargo got her off with minimal damage. All things considered, there was nothing extraordinary about her career to this point.

The details surrounding her last trip are murky. According to the newspapers she left Chicago on September 16, 1856 with a full cargo of wheat. Records are unclear whether she had seven or eight crewmen aboard or even, for that matter, if they were all men. It was common for the schooners to carry a female cook so one of the "men" could have in reality been a female. Regardless, two of the men in the crew didn't want to be aboard at all. In fact reaching Chicago from Buffalo they promptly deserted but at the request of the captain were arrested by the police and returned to the ship. It is likely the men had signed "the articles" in Buffalo for a round trip and the captain was going to hold them to it. Whether they liked it or not, the pair were going where the *Sandusky* did, for better, or worse!

About a week later newspapers carried a small item about a brig foundering in the Straits of Mackinac. Another vessel claimed she sighted the mast of a ship projecting out of the water with eight men hanging on it and reported it to the folks on Mackinac Island. The steamer *Queen City*, enroute to Chicago and laying over at Mackinac, came out to investigate but only found three men still on the mast. The waves were running too high for the steamer to approach the men, so she just steamed off, leaving them to the whim of the gods. The deities were not merciful and all perished.

There was still no positive identification of the wreck however. But as the days passed and more vessels made port the puzzle of information began to make sense. All the evidence pointed to the loss of the *Sandusky*. A report from the steamer *Oriental* saying she sighted the *Sandusky* dismasted near the Beaver Islands confused the situation somewhat.

There was also some talk of a bottle with a note in it found on the beach near Grand River in the southern part of Lake Michigan. The writing was illegible but folks thought they could make out the word "*Sandusky*."

When all the facts were assembled, however soft they were, marine men concluded the wreck in the Straits was the *Sandusky*. She left

SANDUSKY ✳ 5

Chicago, never reached Buffalo and the only unidentified wreck was the one in the Straits, ergo it was the *Sandusky*. Barring an alien abduction theory, it's pretty good logic when you think about it. She was a loss of $18,000.

The mystery was finally solved on May 2, 1981 when enterprising divers from the Ford Seahorses Dive Club discovered her wreck about five miles west of the Straits. The wreck was upright on the bottom and virtually undamaged although her masts were down. Likely the mainmast went off the Beavers as seen by the *Oriental* but the foremast remained upright long enough for the crew to clamber up when she finally sank in the Straits. After the *Queen City* left her, the mast finally gave way, tumbling into the lake, the remaining men having dropped off before or riding it down to their doom.

While the *Sandusky* was a great wreck from a scuba diver's point of view, what made her special was her scrolled figurehead. Great Lakes ships rarely had figureheads of any kind. They were too "work-a-day" to boast such frivolity. The discovering divers documented the wreck thoroughly, which was a good thing indeed, as once the news of the discovery got out hordes of divers swarmed her and one, or perhaps several, attempted to steal her figurehead damaging it in the effort. Perhaps recognizing someone would succeed at stealing it, the figurehead was removed and replaced with a replica. The original is now in a museum.

References:

Chicago Tribune, September 15-17, 1856.

Detroit Advertiser and Tribune, September 1856.

Charles L. Feltner, "Historic Wreck Discovered, What To Do Now?" *Diving Times*, October-November 1981.

Tony Gramer, "*Sandusky* Figurehead Restored," *Diving Times*, Summer 1989, p. 4.

Great Lakes In Depth, November-December 1988.

Cris Kohl, *The Great Lakes Diving Guide* (Chicago: Seawolf Publications, 2008), pp. 356-357.

Mike Kohut, "Firgure Head on *Sandusky* Destroyed." *Diving Times*, Fall 1988, p. 7.

6 ✳ WOOD ON THE BOTTOM

Milwaukee Sentinel, September 23, October 1, 1856.

Stonehouse Collection - *Sandusky*.

Sandusky - www.boatnerd.com.

Straits of Mackinac Shipwreck Preserve - *http://www.michigan-preserves.org/straits.htm*.

✳ **2**

LADY ELGIN

A Deadly Night On The Lake

When the steamer *Lady Elgin* sank on September 8, 1860 with the loss of approximately 350 lives, it was the greatest loss of life on Lake Michigan with the exception of the capsizing of the *Eastland* in the Chicago River in 1915. The *Eastland* killed roughly 841. Like the *Lady Elgin*, the true number will never be known. Also like the *Eastland*, the *Lady Elgin* disaster never should have happened.

The *Lady Elgin* was a double-decked wooden sidewheel steamer built in Buffalo in 1851 by Bidwell, Banta and Company at a cost of $96,000. She was 252-feet long, 33.7-feet in beam and 1,037 tons. Reputedly her engines were taken from the steamer *Cleopatra*, a slaver captured by the U.S. Navy during the Civil War. Some folks claimed using such "tainted" engines cursed the new ship. Regardless of it's history, the engine had a 54-inch cylinder with an 11-foot stroke powering two 32-foot paddlewheels. The steamer was strongly constructed with white oak frames with iron reinforcements and had a capacity of 200 cabin passengers, 100 deck passengers, 43 crew and 800 tons of freight. Initially she was owned by Aaron D. Patchin and Gillman D. Appleby of Buffalo and used to carry passengers and freight along the northern shores of the lakes but when the ports were soon linked by rail, she quickly became redundant and was shifted to general work including excursions. In 1855, the Lake Superior Line of Chicago purchased her. Her final owner was Gordon S. Hubbard & Company of Chicago.

She was named for the wife of Lord Elgin, the Governor General of Canada holding the post from 1847-1854. He is best remembered

The Lady Elgin *in Chicago. Note the large stiffening arches and walking beam steam engine. Author*

for leading the first real attempts to establish responsible government in Canada.

The interior appointments in the *Lady Elgin* were considered excellent and as an added bonus she was also fast. Some travelers thought her beautiful, too. Her tall black stacks and graceful wooden arches added a certain charm to the steamer's lines. She proved a perfect boat for excursions.

The *Lady Elgin* wasn't an especially lucky boat though. In August, 1854 she smashed into an uncharted reef south of Manitowoc, Wisconsin. None of her 300 passengers were injured and she backed off without serious damage. Three years later a fire scorched through the hurricane deck and into her cabins. In the summer of 1858 she was ashore at Copper Harbor on Lake Superior. Originally thought a total loss, she was recovered after several days of work. In August, 1858 she fetched up on Lake Superior's Au Sable Point Reef in a fog sustaining $1400 in damages. Two days later the steamer *Illinois* pulled her free.

Her last cruise left Milwaukee in the early morning of Friday, September 7. Aboard were 400-500 passengers including members of several Milwaukee militia companies including the bulk of the of the

Union Guards, and some of the Black Watch Jaegers, Milwaukee Light Guard and Light Drum Corps, all in full uniform. The Jaegers were formed from Germans who served in the failed rebellion in 1848 against the Prussian government and fled to America to escape prosecution. They were considered to be well trained and efficient militia, the Union Guards especially so. Various city organizations including the city band, fire and police department delegations, city officials and assorted friends and supporters also joined the military men. As the *Lady Elgin* steamed out of the harbor the bands played popular numbers and many of the passengers danced and sang along. After all it was a holiday excursion.

Why the steamer came to have such an unusual passenger list is fascinating in itself and very reflective of the deep political issues that would soon overwhelm the nation.

Milwaukee was a seething cauldron of politics, in many ways mirroring the national concerns of slavery and states rights. Slavery wasn't unknown in Wisconsin, the 1840 census showed 40 slaves in the state. Most were in the southern portion, brought in from Kentucky and Missouri to work the mines. The passage of the Fugitive Slave Act by the Congress in 1850 inflamed local abolitionist tendencies even more than having slaves in the state. The act allowed a U.S. Marshall to obtain a warrant from a federal judge for the arrest of any Negro deemed a fugitive from his lawful master. The slave "owner" only had to claim a Negro, freeman or otherwise to be his escaped property for the act to come into force. The Negro could not even testify in his own defense. The law also provided stiff penalties including fines and jail for anyone guilty of helping a slave to escape. The law went over in Wisconsin like the proverbial "lead balloon."

Regardless of the law, witnesses in Wisconsin commonly testified in favor of the slaves, juries regularly returned verdicts of not guilty and judges dismissed cases on the merest technicality. There were also notable instances of escape from the clutches of the slave catchers. In 1852 Joshua Glover escaped from his master and made his way to Racine where two others escapees joined him. All three eventually took jobs at a local sawmill. In March, 1854 two wagon loads of men including a couple of deputy marshals arrived at his cottage and arrested him but only after a desperate struggle during which they beat him senseless. The following morning marshals dumped him in the Milwaukee jail for safe-keeping. Within a day 100 men from Racine arrived at the jail demanding his release. When the jailer refused to release him, the men broke down the doors with a large wood beam taken from the partially completed St. Johns Cathedral and forcibly took him out. Given a speedy horse he galloped back to Racine, boarded a fast boat and headed for Canada eventually arriving safely. There were other similar cases of escaped slaves being given shelter and escort to freedom in Canada.

Abolitionist fever ran so high in Wisconsin there were rumors the state would secede from the United States if the federal government didn't outlaw slavery. Governor Alexander Randall was a rabid abolitionist and doubtless fed the increasing tension.[1] Things went so far that on March 3, 1860 a member of the Wisconsin legislature introduced a bill directing the governor to declare war on the United States unless Wisconsin's abolitionist demands were met. State Adjutant General J.A. Swain, likely with the knowledge of Randall, sent secret agents to Milwaukee to see whether the city's militia companies would support such a radical move. Would they rally to the state or remain loyal to the United States?

The Union Guards, recruited primarily from the Irish Third Ward and considered the best of the city's four companies, refused to join the treasonous movement. While against slavery, they saw slavery as a proper issue for the national government, not Wisconsin, to deal with. They would not commit treason against their country. In

The uniform of the Union Guard was certainly resplendent. Author

retribution on March 7, 1860 Randall disbanded the Union Guards and revoked the commission of its commander, Garrett Barry. The Adjutant General further directed all state issued arms and equipment be turned over to the Milwaukee Light Guard, a city company apparently more willing to support the secessionist movement, or at least tell the Governor what he wanted to hear. Regardless of the efficiency of the Union Guards, they weren't loyal to the governor and had to go! Hell hath no fury like a politician spurned!

Garry Barry was the popular and efficient commander of the Union Guards. Author

Barry was an anomaly among militia officers in that he not only was a West Point graduate, class of 1839, but also an experienced combat officer. During his Army career he saw action in the Florida War in 1840 and Mexican War 1846-47, serving with distinction at the Battle of Monterey. When he taught infantry tactics at West Point his students included future Union Civil War generals Sherman, McDowell, Thomas, Rosecrans and Grant among others. He resigned from the Army in 1847 to pursue business interests in Milwaukee as a forwarding and commission agent. In 1859 he was elected treasurer of Milwaukee County.

The Union Guards was organized in 1848 as the Milwaukee City Guards under Captain J. McManman. Primarily made up of young Irishmen, the company suffered from a lack of discipline and was reorganized in 1854 under Captain John Jennings as the Milwaukee Union Sarsfield Guards. Jennings was no more successful than McManman in building a disciplined unit and it reorganized a third time in 1856 as the Union Guards. It still suffered from a lack of discipline and two years later Barry took over command and went to work. He selected 50 men out of the old company and recruited another 20 to bring it up to 70 men strong. It didn't take him long to bring the unit to a high state of discipline and efficiency. Barry knew the business of soldiering and passed the hard lessons on to his men, some the "hard" way. Doubtless it was necessary to take a man behind the armory once in a while to "council" him a bit, the miscreant perhaps emerging with a bloody nose and black eye! This was the "Old Army" way to "knock" sense into a difficult recruit. There was a proper time for drinking and carousing and a proper time for soldiering and Barry made certain his men understood the difference! It wasn't long before he drilled them to precision in the manual of arms, cadence, route step, alignment, various marching and parade formations and maneuvers. The company soon gained the reputation of being the "best in the Northwest" and made sojourns to Buffalo, Detroit and Chicago to demonstrate their skill. Often called "Barry's Guards," membership was critical for any young Irishmen wanting to advance in politics or love. Women were always impressed with the sharply turned out guardsmen.

Considering the coming Civil War and the need for good, well-led units like the Barry Union Guards and the idiocy of Wisconsin declaring war on the United States over the issue of slavery, Randall was clearly a dolt to have set out to create the militia havoc he did. I suggest Lincoln recognized Randall's glaring leadership limitations since he appointed him as minister to the Vatican immediately on his departure from the governorship. The Vatican was a good place to put the rapscallion "on ice" for the war years. Lord forbid Randall would ever have an important job!

Governor Alexander Randall, of Wisconsin. He was certainly a contributing factor to the loss. Author

This elevated photo shows the steamers' twin stacks and old style anchors catted forward. Author

The arms for the Wisconsin militia were provided by the federal government but placed under state control, thus the governor (who was expected to be loyal to the federal government, not a potentially traitorous scoundrel like Randall) had the authority to remove them from the company. Without arms the company was a toothless tiger and could be ignored.

The rest of their equipment including uniforms, band instruments, accoutrements as well as armory and furniture were all company owned, paid for by dues and money raised by hosting banquets, picnics and other social functions and fund raisers.

The Union Guards were hopping mad when the governor disarmed them! In a phrase, "They had their Irish up!" Randall had better think again if he thought a pipsqueak like him could break the Union Guards! They felt the governor could take their arms and even officially disband the unit but they could reform as a private independent company with their own arms and equipment, Randall and his cronies be damned! A sympathetic congressman tried to obtain arms directly from the U.S. government but since the unit was no longer part of the militia, was unable to do so unless it paid for them at $2 each.

The men of the company decided they would raise the money with a lake excursion to Chicago on the always popular *Lady Elgin*. The members of the other militia companies as well as city organizations and private individuals were folks who supported the Union Guards and were happy to participate in such a worthwhile trip.

After arriving in Chicago the Union Guards paraded and later everyone went sightseeing in the Windy City including hearing a rousing speech by Illinois Congressman and presidential candidate Stephen A. Douglas at a Democrat party rally.[2] In addition to money raised the excursion helped raise awareness of Randall's high handed action and gained much sympathy.

Later the holidaymakers gathered for a banquet followed by appropriate speechmaking and dancing. By 11:30 p.m. excursionists were back aboard the steamer and the party continued as the steamer pushed north for Milwaukee through freshening northeast wind and waves. The exact passenger count is impossible to determine today but some period newspapers estimated as many as 600 folks could have been on board. (Though 400-500 is more likely.)

Initially the *Lady Elgin's* Captain Jack Wilson was hesitant to leave the dock. The weather seemed to be brewing up and prudence said to remain in Chicago until it blew it self out but passengers were anxious to get home so he departed. He also boarded additional passengers in Chicago bound for Milwaukee and points north so there was some extra pressure to get underway. Wilson was a very experienced master who enjoyed the full confidence of the traveling public. It was an age when captains were not anonymous figures but personalities well known to the community.

About 2:00 a. m. she was buffeted by a powerful squall. Gale force winds blasted the steamer as she churned her way north to Milwaukee. Rain poured down from the heavens in torrents and thunder rumbled across the sky. Occasional bolts of lightning provided an eerie backdrop to the unfolding scene. The stormy weather made little difference to many boisterous passengers who continued to dance, laugh and imbibe. The *Lady Elgin* continued on unbothered by the gale.

The Augusta *striking the* Lady Elgin. *Author*

About seven miles off Winnetka a sudden shudder ran through the steamer. Few of the revelers initially paid much attention to it. They should have since it was her death rattle! Captain Wilson and the first mate George Davis were both asleep in their cabins but quickly gained the deck.

The shutter was caused by the two-masted schooner *Augusta*. Bound from Port Huron to Chicago with a cargo of lumber and commanded by Captain Darius Malott, she smashed into the port quarter of the steamer just aft of the wheel. Witnesses claimed the impact was so severe the bow sliced into the main salon. The two vessels remained together for a minute or so before the schooner broke free. Five minutes later she had drifted off into the black night.

But the steamer was mortally wounded. After slowly rolling hard over to port she gradually came back to a level keel. But the roll extinguished her oil lanterns plunging her cabins and salons into darkness, greatly adding to the confusion among the panicking passengers. Some remained below in their cabins paralyzed by fear. Others stayed through error. One man ordered his wife, daughter and son to remain in their cabin until he found out what was happening. It was a death sentence for his family.

Captain Wilson tried to save the steamer anyway he could. First he jettisoned roughly 150 cattle loaded in Chicago.[3] Trying to force the terror stricken beasts off the ship was easier said then done but eventually many were pushed through the cargo doors and into the lake's tender mercy. Union Guardsmen helped the crew in the effort.

The captain tried to bring the hole in his hull out of the water by having the passengers move to the starboard side of the vessel thus raising up the holed port side. Like the cattle, most were too panic-stricken to cooperate. He had better luck with some iron stoves in the cargo, the crew being able to shove them to the high side to try to raise

Captain Wilson was considered a very competent and experienced captain. Author

the gaping wound out of the water. How effective these efforts were are questionable as some witnesses reported the engine room was holed also.

He also launched two of his three lifeboats with crewmen, supplies of mattresses, blankets and canvas sailcloth. If their crews could work their way around to the hole, perhaps they could plug it long enough to let the ship reach port. Panic again raised its ugly head. One boat only had a single oar and with the crew unable to row to the hole, let the waves drive them to safety ashore. The second boat swamped in the breaking seas and after the crew finally bailed themselves out, discovered the steamer was too far to windward to reach.

In a hopeless effort to signal other vessels, the captain ordered the whistle tied down providing an eerie banshee scream to the storm striven stygian night. No ship save his own heard it.

The Lady Elgin *sinking into Lake Michigan. The lake is covered with the dead and dying. Author*

In a last desperate maneuver he headed the dying ship to shore. Maybe, just maybe, he could find bottom close enough to the beach for his passengers and crew to struggle to safety. It wasn't to be. The surging water flooded the boiler fires and she slowly lost headway. She was just off Winnetka, Illinois.

Frantically people ripped doors off their hinges, tore up planks and benches, all to make hasty life rafts. There were reputedly around 500 life belts aboard, but they were kept in a location later claimed unreachable to passengers.

When the steamer finally sank she went quickly. As common with era vessels, her hurricane deck broke off and for a time floated like a huge raft. An estimated hundred people clambered aboard surviving for some minutes before the waves broke it up into smaller pieces.

Danger makes cowards of some men and heroes of others. When Deputy U.S. Marshall John Horan noticed a woman on the deck raft with her teeth literally chattering from the cold, he gave her his heavy overcoat. She lived while he later died in the breakers.

After the blackness of the gale-whipped night gave grudgingly to a cold dawn, perhaps as many as 400 passengers and crew were bobbing

Two passengers cling desperately to the pilothouse. Author

about on various pieces of the steamer. The lake was still breaking hard and some of the larger deck sections relentlessly broke apart sending their occupants to death in the cold water. Wilson was on one of the larger sections and holding a small child in his arms. When he tried to rig a jury-sail to propel the "raft" toward shore, he passed the child to a woman to hold for him. Mere moments later a large wave swept over the wreckage knocking the child away from the woman to a watery grave.

A couple of the larger hull sections carrying roughly 100 survivors each hung together long enough to reach the shallows near the beach but the pounding waves and steep banks made a mockery of their hopeless efforts to rescue themselves. The powerful waves tore the ad hoc rafts to pieces, throwing survivors into the lake, the same pounding surf dashing them to death against the base of the unforgiving rocks and banks of the shore.

The lifeboat carrying the mate also reached the cliffs but he was able to climb to the top and give the alarm of the wreck. The local railroad telegrapher flashed the news to Chicago. By 8:00 a.m. students from Northwestern University were on site and working to

Survivors held on to anything that floated. Author

haul victims to safety. When folks from Winnetka and nearby Evanston learned of the terrible tragedy unfolding on their doorstep, they hurried to the lakeshore to help. Without proper equipment or training there was little they could do but watch the dreadfulness of death from shipwreck. A total of roughly 160 victims were eventually saved through their own devices or efforts of others. One witness claimed 120 people died less than a hundred feet offshore!

Heroism was commonplace but one Northwestern student stood above all others. Edward W. Spencer is credited with saving 18 lives, time and again going into the breaking surf to pull people to safety despite receiving many injuries from the maelstrom of wreckage surging to and fro in the waves. Known as a great swimmer, he lashed a line around his waist so fellow students could pull him to safety after he grabbed on to a victim. Witnesses claimed he repeatedly asked, "Did I do my best?" According to legend his exertions were so strenuous he became delirious and was confined to a wheelchair for the rest of his life. In 1908 a bronze plaque was unveiled at the Northwestern campus library commemorating his daring rescues.

Charles Beverung, the drummer boy of the Light Guard had the presence of mind to whittle a plug for the air vent of his drum and use

Captain Wilson on a makeshift raft encouraging others to hang on.
Author

it to float ashore. For a while four other folks hung on to the drum too but they gradually weakened and dropped off, sinking forever in the unforgiving lake. Another survivor came ashore by riding the carcass of a cow.

The difficulties faced by survivors once they reached the shore were nearly insurmountable. Along most of the shore were sand banks fully 40 feet high and rocks with waves crashing hard into their base. People who managed against all odds to survive the hungry lake, had to still have the energy and pluck to clamber to safety over rock and bank.

The two captains, Jack Wilson of the *Lady Elgin* and Garrett Barry of the Union Guards, managed to reach the rocks along the shore. Gallant to the end, Wilson is said to have saved two women just before meeting his own death on the rocks. Barry also is said to have helped numerous victims to safety before drowning a bare hundred feet from shore. Barry's son Willie also died in the wreck.

The bedlam on the sinking steamer was matched by that in Milwaukee when word of the disaster reached the city. The telegraph

Edward Spencer and others helped rescue many victims from the deadly surf. Author

offices were deluged with hundreds of shocked relatives and friends seeking word of their loved ones.

It took fully eight weeks for the full magnitude of the disaster to be appreciated. The loss is usually put at 350 people with 160 survivors but these numbers are at best estimates only. It was claimed nearly every family in Milwaukee's Third Ward was affected. Some were literally wiped out. In others only the children survived. Newspapers claimed nearly 1,000 children were orphaned, most in the Third Ward.

Many prominent Milwaukee people died in the wreck including a school commissioner, teachers, city councilor, chief engineer of the fire department, deputy US Marshall, the mayor's clerk, harbor master and register of deeds. Other important folks included F.A. Lumsden, the owner of the *New Orleans Picayune* newspaper, his wife, son and daughter and Herbert Ingraham, a member of the British parliament and owner of the *London Illustrated News* and his 16-year old son.

Once the immediate shock of the disaster passed it was time to fix blame. Someone had to be responsible for the terrible catastrophe!

This wood cut was evidently taken from the picture on page 8. Readers were desperate for news of the wreck and since newspapers were not technologically able to print photos, woodcuts were the order of the day. Author

It started as an artillery duel between rival newspapers. The *Wisconsin Daily Patriot* thundered the blame lay with Governor Randall since he was the one who disarmed and disbanded the pro-federal Union Guards. If it wasn't for his precipitous action, the people would not have made the excursion and thus been lost in the wreck. The rival *Wisconsin State Journal* fired back the real blame was with the editor of the *Daily Patriot* since he so strongly endorsed Randall for the governorship in the first place. If Randall wasn't elected, the disaster would not have happened. Was it the chicken or the egg?

The folks in the street looked at things more directly. Since the *Augusta* hit the *Lady Elgin*, it must be her fault and as Captain Darius Malott was in charge, he was the man to blame. The *Detroit Free Press* defended the captain, since an investigation absolved him of any culpability. The fact the schooner was owned by George Bissell of Detroit certainly played no role in the blame game or the Detroit paper's allegiance to local interests. Not to let the Detroiters get away with a

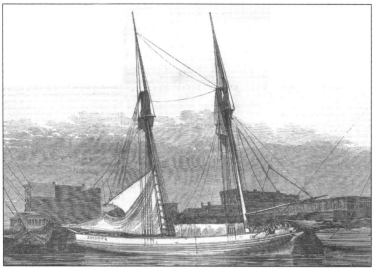

The Augusta *in Chicago after the collision. Note the jury rigged bow
sprit. Author*

faultless defense, the *Milwaukee Journal* fired back, "We know many
lake men who are by no means ready to jump to this conclusion..."

Since passengers from both Chicago and Milwaukee perished on the
wreck both cities held coroners inquests reaching similar conclusions.

Clearly the *Lady Elgin* was overloaded. Too many passengers were
aboard her. When complete passenger lists couldn't be produced, the overloading charge was unchallenged. The cattle only added to the problem.

Both the *Lady Elgin* and *Augusta* had poorly planned navigation
lights. Since seeing another vessel is key to avoiding a collision and
the lights were vital to see another vessel at night, this was obviously
a key factor in the disaster.[4] Malott claimed the *Lady Elgin's* lights
were in the wrong arrangement and when he finally saw her it was too
late to avoid a collision.

Malott, in turn, was castigated for not laying to after the collision to
render possible aid. The captain, though, claimed he didn't know he
caused the steamer any significant damage. He later claimed he didn't
find out about the disaster until he reached Chicago and he and his
crew then went immediately to the authorities to tell their side of the

story. Squaring this assertion when survivors from the *Lady Elgin* stated the schooner's bow smashed through the cabin wall is impossible. His own bow was badly damaged and leaking and foresails torn away. Though unstated, many marinemen thought the captain was lying.

Supposedly, the second mate of the *Augusta* had seen the lights of the steamer well before the collision but failed to tell Malott. The mate, however, swore he did tell Malott. The truth of the matter is, of course, unknown. Malott further claimed the *Augusta* was driving under heavy sail when the squall hit her and his crew was busy trying to reef her

The Augusta *evidently before the collision with the* Lady Elgin. *Institute for Great Lakes Studies*

canvas and regain control when the feeble lights of the steamer suddenly appeared out of the gloom in front of him.

Two of the jurors of a coroner's inquest held Captain Wilson partially liable for failing to post the two lookouts required by his size of ship. Whether the lookouts would have been able to see the dim glow of a schooner's lights in the prevailing storm conditions is problematic.

Regardless of the coroners conclusions, the schooner's owners sided with their captain and assigned him to their bark, *Mojave*. At this point you can whistle the theme to the "Twilight Zone," because the *Mojave* supposedly, disappeared without a trace nearly four years to the day after the *Lady Elgin* loss at a location approximately ten miles from the *Lady Elgin* wreck. Reputedly, all but one of the crew lost on the *Mojave* were on the *Augusta* when she rammed the *Lady Elgin*. Many folks saw the loss as justice. As time passed the loss of the *Mojave* became a bit convoluted and there was even a rumor she foundered in northern Lake Michigan, and just to spice the story up, her crew was lynched in retribution for the *Lady Elgin* "crime."

The local folks, especially those in Milwaukee, placed the blame for the collision squarely on Malott and by extension, the *Augusta*. She became a pariah of sorts, despised wherever she came to port. Legend claims the owners even went so far as to change her name to *Colonel Cook* and repainted her too, all in an effort to disguise her foul past. In 1861 she was sent off on a trip to Liverpool but soon returned to the lakes. Some legends claim she sold saltwater and ended her days far from the lakes but this is incorrect.

The 129-foot *Augusta* was built in 1855 in Oswego by J.A. Baker and named for Augusta Avery, the owner's wife. She was lost in a Lake Erie storm on September 23, 1894. Her crew abandoned her in a sinking condition but the lifeless hulk drifted ashore between Cleveland and Lorain and broke up.

Bodies from the *Lady Elgin* came ashore all along the lake deep into December, some drifting in as far as 80 miles distant. The initial rush of remains were taken by wagonload and special train to the marshal's office in the old Milwaukee courthouse. They were laid out on the bare floor, men, women and children, their calm faces hiding the horror they faced. Some were dressed in finery, others in mere rags

6 ✳ Wood On The Bottom

and remnants of clothing. Regardless, friends and relatives sought
their loved ones out from such bleak surroundings.

Nearly all of the bodies carried some kind of wounds, either
suffered in trying to save themselves or after death in being battered
by the waves. An especially macabre instance was the body of a young
woman less head.

Many were too far gone to be identified ending up in a mass grave
at Winnetka and others on the hillside overlooking the lake. Those that
could be identified were sent home to Milwaukee, their headstones
often bearing the simple inscription "lost on the *Lady Elgin*." One
source estimated perhaps a third of those killed were never recovered,
lost forever in the cold and lonely depths of Lake Michigan.

Captain Wilson's remains were so decayed when finally located, he
was only identified by his gold watch and documents in his pockets. It
was taken to Chicago and a hero's funeral. A great procession
accompanied by a mournful dirge escorted the remains to the train station,
transport to Coldwater, Michigan and internment in the family plot.

Wilson was a 24-year veteran of the lakes and very highly regarded
by both the public and mariners. As was typical for the times he started his career early, shipping out as a deckhand on a schooner before
slowly working his way up to the exalted position of captain. He had
the honor of taking the first steamer through the new Soo Locks in
1855.[5] Wilson owned a farm near Coldwater, Michigan. Located in
roughly the middle of the state and just north of the Indiana border, it
was as distant as possible from the lakes he sailed for so long. His
wife, two daughters and a son kept the farm going in his absence.
Apparently he had dreams of retiring to it someday to live out his days
in bucolic splendor growing apples and peaches. How he could trade
the beauty of the lakes for a mud hole of a bug infested farm in
nowhere Michigan is incomprehensible, but I digress. Following his
death his friends raised sufficient money to pay off the farm's
mortgage and provide something for his survivors to live on.

Captain Barry's body was found along the Indiana shore two
months after the disaster. He had the most imposing funeral of any of
those lost. Much of the city's business shut down for the occasion and
bands played funeral dirges all the way from St. John's Cathedral to
Calvary Cemetery. Considering the splendor of the funeral, and

political issues involved, it is surprising his grave was unmarked at least initially.

Flotsam from the wreck washed ashore for days along a five-mile long stretch of coast and opposite the wreck and many items were hauled away as souvenirs. A large section of hull was on the beach for a number of years and part of the keel was later used to build a barn. For a time her nameboard was displayed in the New Tier High School in Winnetka but eventually disappeared, perhaps tossed away by a historically illiterate administrator.

Governor Randall was cast as a villain in the *Lady Elgin* disaster for disarming the Union Guards and the incident served to further increase the tensions between Democrats and Republicans over the slavery and states' rights issues. An official inquest into the disaster exonerated the captains of the steamer and schooner, finding the rules of lakes navigation in effect at the time to be at fault.

No wreck of the magnitude of the *Lady Elgin* can happen without stories of locals looting the bodies as they came ashore. The dead didn't need the money but the living certainly did, or at least that was the reasoning the ghouls used! Locals claimed thieves from Chicago and Milwaukee not only picked the pockets of the dead but also cut off fingers to remove valuable rings. Authorites caught two thieves trying to make their way off with a trunk belonging to Britisher Herbert Ingraham.

The *Lady Elgin's* bow remained afloat and drifted until her dragging anchors finally caught several miles off Winnetka. Slowly she settled to the bottom. The upside down hull section remained a hazard to navigation for some time after the accident until it finally sank.

One of the mysteries of the wreck involves a strange steamer hove to about ten miles offshore for about three hours. It was during the height of the gale and observers on shore could clearly see her but she made no effort to try to aid any of the folks in the water but just kept her bow sea on and watched. Later she came within three miles of shore but still gave no assistance to any of the victims. Later it turned out she was the tug *McQueen* and no explanation was ever given of her failure to help those drowning around her.

The last survivor of the *Lady Elgin* disaster was Albert Doebert, a member of the City Band, succumbing on November 10, 1921.

Even today, a century and a half after the wreck, she is still the subject of occasional newspaper and magazine articles. For a generation after the disaster she was the topic of many stories, songs, poems and art pieces. The most famous song, "Lost on the *Lady Elgin*," was written by Henry C. Work, best known for the old Civil War favorite, "Marching Through Georgia." In today's terms the *Lady Elgin* was "hot." Since the majority of the Union Guards were parishioners of the St. John Cathedral in Milwaukee, the church held a memorial service on the following September 8th, a tradition continuing to this day.

On St.Patrick's Day, 1996, an historical marker commemorating the disaster was placed at the corner of North Water and Erie Streets in Milwaukee's Third Ward by the Wisconsin State Historical Society.

It can be weakly argued some good did come of the wreck. In 1873 the lighthouse at Grosse Point was erected complete with a powerful 2nd order Fresnel lens. While the light certainly aided mariners in determining their relative position to shore, there is no reason to think the light would have prevented the collision on that dark and stormy

The U.S. Life-Saving Service Station at Evanston was established in 1878 on the campus of Northwestern University and student manned. Ted Richardson Collection

The lighthouse at Grosse Point was established in 1873, even if it had been operational on the night of the disaster, it would have been of no practical value. Author

night a generation before. Of more practical value was the U.S. Life-Saving Service Station established at Northwestern University in 1878. Had a Life-Saving Service crew been available doubtless more lives would have been saved, but the scope of the disaster was so massive even their professional effort would have been far, far too little to meet the need. The *Lady Elgin* was just one on a list of wrecks used to justify the establishment of a station at Evanston.

Unlike most Great Lakes shipwrecks the *Lady Elgin* did not go quietly into the night other than her remembrance in song and service.

In the mid 1970s Chicago salvor Harry Zych began to search for the wreck. Using side scan sonar and proton magnometers, huge areas of the lake floor were swept looking for the steamer. In 1989 he found her and the old steamer was soon the centerpiece of another storm.

Zych wanted to recover artifacts from the wreck for a traveling exhibit for the general public. The State of Illinois through the Illinois

Historic Preservation Agency took exception to this effort, claiming ownership and stating a desire to leave artifacts on the bottom for "archeological study." The issue entered the Alice in Wonderland world of litigation eventually following the yellow brick road from bench to bench and judge to judge until a federal court finally awarded Zych legal ownership of the wreck. Some artifacts including muskets, swords, glassware, china, serving ware, ship's whistle and a chandelier have been recovered for public display by his nonprofit organization, The *Lady Elgin* Foundation.[6]

The battle lasted seven long years before the court finally gave title to the long suffering Zyck. The decision ultimately turned on whether the insurance company, Aetna (now Cigna) had ever abandoned the wreck. Aetna paid Hubbard (ship owner) $12,000 following the loss thus still owned her. At one point a deal was reached between the Illinois Historic Preservation Committee and Zych that would have given title to the state but allowed Zych finders credit, compensation and a position on a wreck oversight committee. But when the state violated the agreement Zych again turned to the court for relief. In court the state argued that since Aetna and its subsequent companies had done nothing to recover the wreck in the intervening 135 years they had in fact abandoned it. The judge disagreed with the state. Since Aetna had six letters in their files showing they had taken title, the burden was on the state to prove Aetna had indeed abandoned her, stating, "abandonment cannot be presumed by the passage of time or non-use."

What is left of the *Lady Elgin* is in four main wreckage fields several miles off Highwood, Illinois. Perhaps the area of most interest is the bow section which is broken in 60 feet of water. Another debris field contains her boiler and yet a third, her sidewheels. As in other Great Lakes wrecks, divers have stolen a considerable amount of the loose artifacts.

In common with other notable shipwrecks the *Lady Elgin* has her share of premonition tales. One involves Herbert Ingraham, the owner of the *Illustrated London News*. It seems he had several premonitions against making the trip but not wanting to be considered a coward, ignored them and boarded the steamer. There is also a story the Ingraham family was cursed by an Egyptian mummy. It seems his father purchased a mummy in Egypt and sent it to the British Museum for "unrolling." During the deciphering process it was found to contain a curse stating anyone who disturbed the mummy would die a horrible death and his body would be always swept by the sea. Of course the curse was scoffed at but within a year Herbert's younger brother Walter was trampled to death by an elephant he wounded when hunting in Somaliland. His brother's body was temporarily buried in what was thought to be a stone valley but when Herbert returned to bring it home, it couldn't be found. The supposedly dry valley was really a streambed, dry during the hot season. When the rains came the body was washed away. Herbert's own death on the *Lady Elgin* fit the curse perfectly, too, as did that of his son's.

Mrs. Lumsden, the wife of F.A. Lumsden of the *New Orleans Picayune* also reputedly had a premonition about the *Lady Elgin* and didn't want to board the ship. However, her husband insisted and after cajoling, she reluctantly boarded the ship. Captain Wilson also wanted to stay in Chicago that night but his lack of enthusiasm was likely more weather driven than supernatural.

Regardless of supernatural intervention or not, the steamer *Lady Elgin*, caught in the currents of national polictics and intrigue, buffeted by a lake gale and smashed by the cleaving bow of a poorly lighted schooner, perished with the loss of perhaps 350 lives. It was a harbinger of the national tragedy yet to come.

References:

Association for Great Lakes Maritime History, February 1989; May 1993.

C. Patrick Labadie, "Letters" *Inland Seas*, Spring 1991.

Chips, November 13, 1889; January 21, October 14, 1991; December 7, 1992 September 20, 1993; October 4, 1993, April 1, June 24, 1996.

David J. Cooper, "Letters" *Inland Seas*, Winter 1991.

Institute for Great Lakes Research, Bowling Green State University.

J.B Mansfield, *History of the Great Lakes*, (Chicago, 1899), p. 689.

Chicago Tribune, May 7, 1996.

Detroit Free Press, September 12, 1860; August 29, 1878.

Lady Elgin File - Stonehouse Collection.

Milwaukee Sentinel, September 2, 1854; October 30, 1857 November 17, 27, 1858; August-October, December 13, 22, 1860.

Nor'Easter, Journal of the Lake Superior Marine Museum, September-October 1990; September-October 1991; July-August 1996.

Runge Collection, Wisconsin Marine Historical Society.

Charles M. Scanlan, *The* Lady Elgin *Disaster* (Milwaukee, 1928), pp. 12-13, 21-22. 33-35. 38-39. 44. 51-52, 73-74.

Wisconsin Daily Patriot, March 10, September 10, 11, 13, 1860.

Wisconsin State Journal, September 8, 10, 11, 17, 1860.

Wreck of *Lady Elgin* -http://www.ship-wrecks.net/shipwreck/projects/elgin/

Dr. John L. Mahar, "One Hundredth Anniversary of the *Lady Elgin*," *Inland Seas*, Spring 1960, pp. 4-13.

Alexander Randall - Wikipedia.Com.

June Skinner Sawyers, *Chicago Sketches, Urban Tales, Stories and Legends*, (Wild Onion Books: Chicago 1995), pp. 169-170.

Recollections of Wisconsin slaves by pioneer settlers - http://www.wisconsinhistory.org/turningpoints/search.asp?id=1559

Superiorland, October 15, 1994.

Footnotes:

[1] Randall served from 1858-61. He created a camp for assembling Wisconsin Civil War troops in Madison named "Camp Randall." It was later absorbed by the University of Wisconsin and the present football stadium is named in his honor.

[2] There is some doubt whether they heard Douglas or not.

[3] Sources differ on the number of cattle, ranging from "a few" to 150. Regardless, they added weight to the ship and were very difficult to manage in the aftermath of the collision.

[4] The critical importance of vessels showing clearly visible and understood navigational lights would appear to be self evident. It wasn't

then and still isn't today especially among small craft operators. One only has to stand on a dock at night in a busy public launch ramp to see the large number of boats with one or more dysfunctional navigation lights. Even worse are kayakers. Often referred to by boaters as "painted logs," their operators are sometimes incredibly arrogant regarding the need to display any kind of lights at all at night. I once watched a husband and wife paddling their logs happily along a very busy waterway at night in the midst of heavy recreation traffic with nothing more than a very dim battery powered lantern strapped to the rear of the kayaks. The fact that the light was very low to the water and the kayakers body blocked 180 degrees of its arc bothered them not at all. And when some poor boater runs these two miscreants over, he will be blamed for not keeping an adequate watch. Instead he should be given an award for improving the gene pool. But I digress.

[5] *Illinois*

[6] The *Lady Elgin* case is fascinating on a number of levels. In particular it starkly shows the mindset of the publicly paid underwater archeologists demanding Zych turn the wreck over to them for study claiming it was a "publicly owned cultural resource." Their selfserving attitude was that he could risk his time, money and talents to find the wreck but then had to turn it over to them without even a "thank you, Sir". That Zych could potentially earn a "profit" from his hard work was abhorrent to them. Understand, none of these publicly paid academics had ever actually searched for the wreck or had any plans to do so. This same situation plays itself out every time a major shipwreck is discovered by private citizens. The publicly paid vultures attack in an effort to wrest the prize away from the risk takers.

✳ 3

ORIOLE

Cut Down In The Fog

The Lake Superior mines, especially those in the Marquette Range, provided some of the richest iron ore ever discovered in America. Initially found in 1844 it, together with the copper in the Keweenaw Peninsula, set off a mineral "rush" as electrifying as the more famous California rush five years later. Men from the lower lakes as well as east coast came packing to stake out their fortune in iron. During the Civil War the Marquette Range provided the great bulk of the iron for the Union. Area iron mines continue to produce today.

The problem was moving it to market, or in this case, to the iron and steel mills on Lake Erie. Hauling it by ship was the most efficient method but since the mines were located 20 miles or so inland from the port of Marquette, transportation and handling were critical.

The ore emerged from the deep shaft mines on a small rail cart called a tram and then loaded to special rail cars for transportation to the docks in Marquette Harbor. Also known as "pocket" docks, the structures allowed railcars to run on to the dock trestle to dump the raw iron ore into large internal pockets for temporary storage. When the ship moored to the docks, chutes were lowered and the ore rumbled into the holds. Unloading was a laborious process, mostly accomplished by men using hand shovels and wheelbarrows.

In the early days, before the shipyards started turning out specialized bulk freighters, the ore went to the mills by schooner.

The 141-foot, 323-ton, three masted schooner *Oriole,* under Captain Daniel McAdams, departed Marquette at 8:00 p.m. Friday,

The steamer Illinois *cut the schooner down in the fog off Grand Island*. *Marine Collection - Milwaukee Public Library*

August 8, 1862 bound for Erie, Pennsylvania with a full load of iron ore. Aboard were nine crewmen, one passenger, the captain's wife plus his mother-in-law, for an ominous total of 13 souls. According to old sailing superstition a trip should never start on a Friday, especially not one with 13 people aboard. But business is business and the ore was due in Erie as quickly as it could be delivered. Who had time for old superstitions anyway?

At 7:00 a.m. the next day the wooden sidewheel steamer *Illinois* arrived in Marquette with her bow shattered from keel to upper deck. The crew said she struck an unknown schooner in the fog several miles off North Light on Grand Island. They claimed when she was first sighted, the schooner was running directly toward the steamer and had she continued on course would have struck the *Illinois* amidships. The steamer sheared off in an attempt to avoid a collision resulting in ramming the schooner on her quarter.

Questioned by local marine men, the *Illinois* passengers reported hearing screams in the water following the collision and had supposed the schooner had gone down. They severely criticized the steamer's Captain Ryder for not stopping to help the sinking wind wagon and claimed the *Illinois* wasn't even blowing her fog whistle. Others

The schooner Midnight *at a Marquette ore dock (aka "pocket" dock) in early spring. She was similar to the lost* Oriole. *Author*

aboard, including a Bishop McCoskey, claimed that while he heard voices, he didn't think them cries for help.[1]

The mystery of what schooner she hit wasn't solved until Monday afternoon when the steamer *Globe* under Captain J.H. Clifford came into port. Aboard was Andrew P. Fleming of Sodus, New York, the cook from the *Oriole*. The *Globe* picked him up drifting helplessly in the schooner's yawl about six miles from shore at 8:00 p.m. Sunday.

When the cook was interviewed he was still in tough shape with swollen limbs from 40 hours exposure but he was able to tell a damning tale of disaster. He said he crawled into his bunk at a quarter past midnight on the 8th. At the time the schooner was running in fog but it wasn't so thick the signal lamps in the mastheads couldn't be seen from deck. The mate and three sailors were on watch. Four other sailors were asleep in the forecastle and everyone else in the aft cabin. Without warning at 3:00 a.m. the steamer struck the *Oriole* on her starboard quarter, cutting deep into Fleming's cabin and literally slicing the schooner in half! When the stern broke off as a solid piece, the cook was thrown into the water. Hanging onto a piece of wood from the cabin he looked back and saw the remarkable sight of the schooner still under full sail, but minus her stern! Seeing the steamer about 50 feet away, he called for help but received no answer. Looking back again toward the schooner he watched as she disappeared into the gray gloom. When he looked back to the steamer she too was gone into the fog.

For a time he bobbed around in a sea of flotsam including several trunks and a half dozen women's dresses. All the while he could hear another voice out in the night. The disembodied voice lasted for about an hour and a half and then all was silent save the lapping of the cold waves.

Shortly after the wreck Fleming also heard the whistles of another steamer apparently following close behind the *Illinois*. Later he

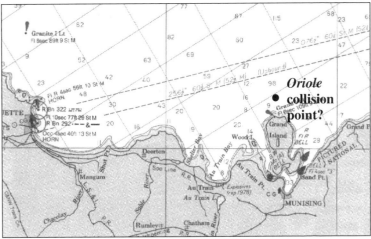

General location.

learned it was likely the *Sea Bird*. She continued on without realizing what happened. About 8:00 a.m. Fleming found the *Oriole's* still floating stern. After paddling over to it he crawled aboard and launched the yawl still hanging from the davits, but without oars he just drifted helplessly until picked up by the *Globe*. The stern continued to drift for a considerable period of time and was later found on the north shore of the lake.

The *Lake Superior News and Journal*, the local Marquette newspaper, criticized Captain Ryder of the *Illinois* for not stopping and rescuing the schooner's survivors. The captain was defended by his clerk, Mr. Atlwood, who reminded the public Ryder's first duty was to his own vessel and the safety of his 150 passengers. One of them was the illustrious Mayor Duncan of Detroit.[2] Both Duncan and Bishop McCloskey later published a card in the *Detroit Free Press* exonerating Captain Ryder from any blame for the accident.

According to the clerk, the captain was asleep when the collision occurred and the force of it woke him. Rushing on deck he immediately determined the extent of his own injury. After being lowered by rope over the bow to closely examine the damage, Duncan McEachen, an old and experienced sailor, told the captain they would fill in 30 minutes. Fearing for the safety of his passengers after such an ominous report, Captain Ryder headed the *Illinois* toward shore for about half an hour until closer examination of the damage showed he was in no danger of sinking and could safely continue for Marquette. A single pump was able to handle the water gushing in through the bow. The captain kept the knowledge of the damage from the passengers to avoid panic.

Meanwhile First Mate Thomas Wilson, on watch at the time of the collision, supposedly told the captain the schooner "appeared not much injured." He said from her direction he thought she was upbound and light (running without cargo). Running empty would make her more buoyant and less likely to sink.

Captain Ryder could have been thinking of another schooner-steamer collision two years before. It would be remarkable if he wasn't doing so. When the schooner *Augusta* and steamer *Lady Elgin* collided off Winnetka, Illinois on Lake Michigan in August, 1860 the result was terrifying. Approximately 350 souls perished when the steamer sank. It would be hard to believe Captain Ryder didn't let the *Lady Elgin* disaster affect his decision to run for safety rather than worry about a schooner with perhaps a dozen folks aboard.

The clerk also said the fog wasn't consistent but rather in banks. Just before the collision the *Illinois* left a clear area and thus wasn't blowing a fog whistle but neither was the schooner. Regardless of the explanations offered, the local bitterness toward the *Illinois* was considerable. No one could understand why, once he assured himself his ship wasn't sinking, he didn't return and look for survivors from the schooner.

Off Whitefish Point, the propeller *Backus* recovered numerous items from a wreckage field including the schooner's wooden secretary containing her books and papers, a quantity of women's clothing, one gold watch, a lady's purse holding $48, some jewelry and several daguerreotypes of the captain, his wife and children.

Surprisingly, Captain MeLeod of the schooner *Plover* discovered part of the schooner's deck still floating eight miles north of the Pictured Rocks. Climbing aboard and closely examining the wreck, he reported the "hull was cut in two, with the bottom out and masts, sides, spars and part of the deck with sails and rigging floating on the surface." The hat worn by the captain's wife when she was last in Marquette was the only trace of any person discovered aboard. Captain McLeod stated the wreck was one of the saddest sights he had ever seen. He, like many others, was most critical of the performance of the officers of the *Illinois*.

Mate Thomas Wilson, on watch when the collision occurred, had his officer's papers taken immediately following the disaster by the Steamboat Inspection Service officers in Detroit. After due investigation he was exonerated of the blame and his "ticket" was restored to him in October, 1862.[3]

The *Oriole*, with her cargo of 501 tons of iron ore was a loss of $17,000. She was built in Milan, Ohio by Merry and Gay in 1857. The *Illinois*, under Captain Jack Wilson, was famous as the first ship to transit the Soo Locks upbound on June 18, 1855. Wilson was later captain of the *Lady Elgin* when lost in collision with the schooner *Augusta*.

References:

Alexander Meakin, *Master of the Inland Seas* (Vermilion, Ohio: Great Lakes Historical Society, 1888) pp. 5-7.

Bernie Arbic and Nancy Steinhaus, *Upbound Downbound, The Story of the Soo Locks* (Sault Ste. Marie: Chippewa County Historical society, 2005), p. 21

Oriole File - Stonehouse Collection.

Oriole - www.Boatnerd.com

Detroit Mayors - 1701-2001 - http://www.historydetroit.com/people/people.asp?names

Lake Superior News and Journal (Marquette, Michigan), August 15, 22, September 5, 1862.

Portage Lake Mining Gazette, August 16, 23, 30, September 13, 1862.

Wells List, p. 5.

Footnotes:

[1] McCoskey was a bishop of an undetermined Protestant denomination in Detroit.

[2] Duncan was mayor from 1862-63 and a state senator 1863-64.

[3] There is some confusion on the identity of the mate but it appears the same Thomas Wilson who became one of the great ship owners and operators on the lakes with the "Wilson Fleet." The sources show he was the mate on the steamer *Mineral Rock* in 1862 moving to the *Illinois* the following year. However, it wouldn't be unusual for the records to be off by a year or not account for a temporary assignment. Assuming he was on the *Illinois*, he was present as captain when the propeller *Meteor* struck the propeller *Pewabic* in August, 1872, in Lake Huron sinking her with the loss of an estimated 100 lives. Since the mate was on watch when the ships collided, it was the mate who went on trial for manslaughter. He was acquitted.

✳ 4

ALVIN CLARK
Triumph And Tragedy

Perhaps no single instance in Great Lakes maritime history so magnificently demonstrates the triumph of an individual and utter failure of the official historical preservation system than the tragedy of the schooner *Alvin Clark*. In spite of the many folks and organizations that assisted him and his crew there should be no doubt the single driving force was Frank Hoffman whose indomitable spirit overcame all obstacles save one.

When she was built in Trenton (Truago) Michigan in 1846, she was just a normal work-a-day Great Lakes schooner indistinguishable from perhaps a thousand others. At a 105-feet long and 218-feet in beam, she was a bit on the smallish side as follow-on sailing vessels grew bigger and bigger. Cargos of hay, brick and salt and other bulk freight were her lifeblood. Salt was a more important cargo than we are prone to realize, as it was vital at the time to preserve not only meat, but fish too. Hauling salt from lower lakes ports like Oswego and Buffalo to the great fisheries of Lake Michigan would have been common during the early part of her career. Once the Michigan salt industry started in the early 1850s thus negating bringing it up from the lower lakes, she likely left the trade and was sold to G.W. Bissell of Detroit.

Bissell also used her for a variety of other bulk cargos including grain, coal, lumber and still an occasional load of salt. She was in all respects a sea-going truck hauling whatever needed hauling to where ever it needed to be hauled and doing it as cheaply as possible. One way to economize was to provide only the barest minimum of crew.

Where perhaps seven or even more men was more common for a Great Lakes sailing craft during this period, she often sailed with only five and not all the five were real sailors. A couple of "sailors" could be landsmen just working their passage on her. A sailor's wage wasn't much either. In the early 1850's $13 a month was the going rate for a man without the special skills of a carpenter or mate. With close attention to the bottom line, carrying as much cargo as could be crammed aboard as fast as feasible, minimizing crew size and paying them as little as possible, building and maintaining her to the minimal standard necessary, schooners like the *Clark* could show a handsome annual profit. For example, in 1852 she had a net return of nearly $1,700 on freights of $6,841.15 and expenses of $5,142.03.

In the spring of 1856 she was sold to Captain William Higgie of Racine. His nephew Francis B. Higgie crewed aboard her for three years, leaving in 1859 to take command of the schooner *Lewis B. Irwin*. Early on, Francis became embroiled in the slavery issue. Many of the small Wisconsin ports were connected to the "Underground Railroad" and runaway slaves sometimes were discovered in the state by Southern slave catchers. By federal law, local authorities were bound to assist in their return south as they were considered nothing more than stolen property although in this instance the "property" stole itself! Although the circumstances are shadowy apparently Francis, though a mere lad of 16, was forced to assist the sheriff in capturing and turning a runaway over to the slave catchers. Adding confusion to the situation local abolitionists adamantly fought to prevent the sheriff from doing his lawful duty. It wasn't quite anarchy but in some situations came close. It was also a battle that was playing itself out in countless Northern towns and villages and certainly a warning bell of the horror or the coming Civil War. It was an experience that made Francis abhor the whole idea of slavery. After mastering a number of ships, Francis went on to a career as vessel agent and shipbroker.

Under Captain William Higgie, the *Alvin Clark* primarily hauled lumber from Manistee, Michigan to Chicago. Manistee was one of the great centers of the Michigan white pine trade. The lumber barons of Manistee (and Michigan in general) were some of the most unscrupulous operators and miscreants the Great Lakes ever saw. They were our version of Caribbean pirates but instead of plundering from ships at sea or sacking ports, they just stole the public's timber. At the time most of Michigan was public land and great stands of white pine dominated the landscape. Instead of buying the timber rights from the government, the lumber barons just cut away, shipping the valuable lumber to market and leaving a wasteland of slashing and destruction behind. Federal timber agents were virtually nonexistent. Once when an agent tried to enforce the law, the lumber barons reportedly arranged for him to suffer from a deadly case of lead poisoning. Other times a good beating or dose of tar and feathers did the trick. Should a baron actually be arrested for his thieving against the public, corrupt judges just dismissed the charges. It is amusing that today many of the old lumber towns have libraries, theaters and other public buildings named in honor of the crooks who stole so blatantly from the American public. Of course the pirates paid for the buildings late in life as a way of "rehabilitating" shattered reputations and salving guilty conscious.[1]

William Higgie was apparently up to his eyeballs in the illicit trade, not only in Manistee but nearby Grand Haven too. There is evidence

Many schooners hauled lumber from Manistee, Michigan, to market in Chicago. In the early days, much of it was stolen from federal lands. In this photo the schooner Isabella Sands *is being towed up the Manistee River by a tug. Author*

the *Alvin Clark* was in Grand Haven during a battle with federal agents resulting in Higgie being arrested and tossed in the local jail. His loyal crew attacked the lock-up, breaking him out and taking back their cargo of stolen lumber the federal agents confiscated. Higgie sold the hot lumber in Chicago. Arrested again in Manistee, he reputedly bribed his way out of jail and quickly left town with another load of stolen lumber. The piracy continued until 1877 and the administration of Republican Rutherford Hayes. Secretary of the Interior Carl Schurz energetically prosecuted the pirates and removed corrupt officials but by then most of the great stands of white pine were gone and pirates moved west to the Pacific Northwest.

By any measure the *Alvin Clark* is part of the rich maritime history of the Great Lakes. Whether she carried salt, coal, grain or stolen lumber she was busy earning her keep. And when she sank in a squall in Green Bay it didn't cause much of a stir either. Sailing ships sank all the time. Why was her loss any different?

On June 29, 1864 the *Clark* was bound from Chicago for Oconto, Wisconsin to load lumber. Chicago was growing rapidly and Wisconsin wood was critical to keep the businesses and homes building. For a time, until the great forests were harvested, Oconto was a major port in the trade. The trip was good so far; two days out and she was off Chambers Island in Green Bay. The *Clark* was moving well under all sail, already having worked her way through the notorious "Death's Door Passage" at the northern tip of the Door Peninsula. Today the bones of perhaps a hundred vessels litter the area, overwhelmed by gale and storm or smashed on the guarding reefs and shoals. Oconto lay west of Chambers Island and 50 miles or so south from the dangerous passage.

The schooner was marginally manned with only Captain Durnin, Mate Dunn, two able seamen and a fellow working off his passage home to Oconto. Ominously, her hatch covers were off so the hold could air out. The weather was good so what was the danger? Three other vessels were nearby and all were under full canvas too.

About 4:30 p.m. the winds became a bit "fluky," not clearly blowing from any consistent direction. Captain Durian also likely noticed what looked like a rain shower dancing across the lake towards him. It was no matter. A little rain didn't hurt anyone. But it wasn't a

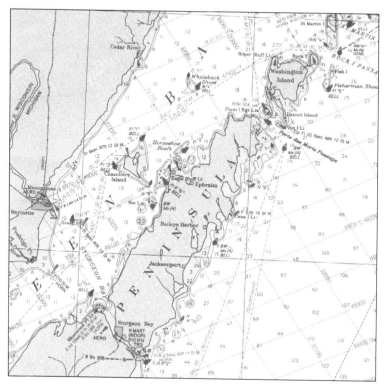

little rain. Instead, a full fledge squall slammed hard into her and with all sails set she was easy prey. The blast snapped her topgallant and broke the topmast for good measure. A second gust hammered her over on her beam ends. With her hatches off, the lake poured into her empty hold. She was a dead ship but still afloat. A nearby schooner, the *Dewitt*, saw the accident and managed to rescue the two crewmen, the only survivors.

It is entirely possible Francis Higgie was aboard the *Dewitt* as captain. In 1862, he purchased an interest in schooner *William H. Dewitt* with his uncle and sailed her for four seasons. Assuming the schooners are one and the same, then Higgie may have watched his old ship capsize!

The *Clark*, however, didn't immediately sink. Rather, it was discovered a couple days later in 50 feet of water with her stern on the surface. The owners, William and John Higgie, quickly sent a tug to haul her into shallow water. Given time she could be raised, pumped out and returned to service. The salvors were too late. When they arrived the schooner was gone, sunk in water deep enough to hide her masts. The theory was the great weight of her anchors and chains pulled the bow and eventually stern down and when she waterlogged, dropped to the bottom. Until then she "ghosted" along partly submerged and partly surfaced finally reaching deep water and disappearing.

A schooner lost in a knock down on Lake Michigan was nothing unusual and was soon forgotten. The Civil War soon ended and in the spasm of national exultation folks looked forward, not backward. There was no interest in the *Alvin Clark.*

But everything changed in November, 1967 when commercial fisherman Dick Garbowski asked his friend, diver Frank E. Hoffman, to clear whatever obstruction his nets were fouled on 110 feet below the chilly waters of Green Bay. The nylon net was worth $1,400 and couldn't just be abandoned. Garbowski tried to free it with his tug the *Dellie W.* by pulling in various directions but the net was stuck fast. Garbowski was certain the net was fouled on a wreck. After leaving the net on a buoy he ran over the area several times with his sonar tracing out what looked to him like a shipwreck.

Frank owned the Anchor Inn bar and a small resort motel in the community of Egg Harbor on Wisconsin's Door Peninsula. The 80-off mile long peninsula forms the eastern arm of Green Bay.

Garbowski called Hoffman on Wednesday, November 1, but since Hoffman was working construction in Milwaukee, he wasn't able to dive immediately but promised to take a look on the coming weekend. Hoffman tried to convince divers he knew from Chicago and Madison to take the dump with him but none were available on such short notice. He would have to dive alone. Today diving alone is viewed by the scuba community as an absolute prohibition, an utterly reckless thing to do. But in the 1960s it wasn't considered unusual.

It was far too rough to dive on Saturday and Sunday was just marginally better. Cold winds whistled across the bay and the *Dellie W.* "rocked and rolled" in the sharp chop. But Hoffman suited up in his old wetsuit, strapped on a tank, added a couple of knives and grasping a non-too reliable underwater light, splashed into the water.

As he descended the murky water grew colder and darker. The feeble yellow beam from his light reached out a mere six feet or so. At about 100 feet the beam flickered across the rail of the wreck. He could just make out a row of deadeyes through the shadowy gloom.

On this first dive Hoffman found two things. First he needed a lot of help to free the net and second, it was tangled on the bowsprit and catheads of a very old wood vessel.[2] From what little he could see in the terrible visibility she was a remarkable discovery. Since initially her name was a mystery, she soon acquired the title of the "Mystery Ship from Nineteen Fathoms." From his examination she was also intact with no evidence of structural damage.

The fishermen had no interest in the wreck. They just wanted the net. Great Lakes wrecks aren't Spanish treasure galleons overflowing with gold doubloons and jewels, so why bother with it?

Hoffman assembled a group of divers and they tackled the nets every weekend until December. It was miserable diving. Visibility was horrible, bottom silt easily stirred up, the water cold and air colder. This was wet suit diving at it's worst. Dry suits, as commonly used today, were far in the future and quarter inch thick neoprene wet suits were the standard. The theory was a thin layer of water would enter between the divers's skin and suit. Over time the diver's own body heat would warm the water and he would be nice and comfy. It was a dream! The suits rarely fit well so the "thin" layer of water was in reality a very thick one constantly pulling heat from the diver. The suits often ripped allowing more water to enter. Worst of all, at 115 feet down the quarter inch of insulating neoprene became paper thin from compressed providing minimal insulation. Most of the suits weren't even custom, just purchased off the rack as large, medium or small. Everyone knows how well standard sizes actually fit! Divers emerged after 20 minutes on the bottom shaking with cold.

While getting the nets free was the job at hand, the divers couldn't help but sneak a look at the wreck. She was sitting upright on the bottom, giving the impression she could just sail away if only sails still graced the yards. Her anchors hung from the pockets and booms on the deck. Since the running and standing rigging had long ago rotted away the deck was littered with blocks, pulleys and deadeyes.[3]

When the icy blasts of winter finally drove the divers off the lake they began to research the schooner's identity. After digging around in the records it became likely she was the *Alvin Clark*. A story in the *Green Bay Advocate* of July, 1864 best described her demise. "She was struck by a squall such as we seldom get in this quarter, tearing up trees by the roots and downing fences, picking up the water before it and carrying it for hundreds of feet ahead. The schooner was caught in the unexpected storm and capsized while under full sail. Three of the crew drowned while two members managed to be picked up by another ship."

Although the divers were able to identify her and eventually the media picked up the tale, she always was called the "Mystery Ship." *Alvin Clark* just didn't have any punch!

Perhaps the idea came to them over a cold beer or two during the winter but it wasn't long before the divers began to think about the opportunity to raise the schooner. Why not? She looked to be in terrific shape. Why, if we got her up maybe we can even sail her! It was, by any measure, an incredibly stupid idea.

Not one of the diving crew had the slightest knowledge of marine salvage or even the trials and tribulations of professional diving. They were sport divers, weekend aquanauts. In the real world or work they were tavern keepers, electronic engineers and the like. A more unsuitable bunch of salvors couldn't be imagined.

Practicing "due diligence" they asked the professionals for advice. Some was useless and some informative. Most questioned their sanity and called the thought of raising the schooner "impossible."

It is said that, "fools go forth where brave men fear to tread," and ignoring the experts, the divers took a vote and decided they would do the impossible. After all, this was their chance to make a tremendous contribution to Great Lakes maritime history. The risks were balanced out by the gain. To make certain things were done "Bristol Fashion," Hoffman obtained title and salvage rights to the schooner.[4]

In the spring of 1968 they went to work and found it was a far larger job than they initially thought. Work days were 16 hours long and ran seven days a week. The weeks piled up into months and the months into years. Two very long hard years passed before they were successful.

———————

Frank Hoffman, (back to camera) holding a block recovered by a diver. Note the head mounted work light, old fashioned 1/4-inch neoprene suit and archaic "life-vest". Author

Working bottom time at 110 feet was only 20 minutes, the maximum without having to decompress. Nitrogen narcosis and the bends were major potential problems. Having to "hang off" the line at a given depth decompressing underwater meant more time exposed to the numbing cold. After finishing a dive it was necessary to stay on the surface for three hours to allow the body to shed the nitrogen in the blood before diving again. This all meant divers could only do three dives every other day alternating with a two dive day. This was long before the popular dive computers of today so the Navy Dive Tables were the controlling authority. Safety was always paramount.

Water temperature hovered around 36-42 degrees and the dives were hard working dives, pushing, pulling, cutting etc. A 60-foot surplus military landing craft provided by Marinette Marine Corporation was their surface base of operations. Named *Cleo*, she was

The barge Cleo *was critical to supporting diving operations. Author*

a critical piece of equipment for the amateur salvors. She was big enough to carry their pumps, compressors, dive equipment and crew. The small cabin also slept four and had a stove, refrigerator, running water and heat. Compared to what they were using, *Cleo* was the *Queen Mary* with all the amenities!

Visibility was miserable. Even with lights it was difficult to punch through the darkness to see what you were doing, or more properly, "trying" to do. Seeing two feet was perhaps average. Once divers began working and disturbing the mud on the deck and in her cabin and hold, visibility dropped to near zero. Using a large suction pump the mud was slowly removed from the wreck but it took months to finish the job.

Divers recovered hundreds of small artifacts including dishes, pottery, bottles, oil lamps, navigation instruments, clothing, boots, a double barreled shotgun and powder horn, clay pipes, coins, galley stove, etc. A surprising find was a crock of 15 pounds of cheese. It was still edible and was claimed to be the oldest edible cheese in the world. The schooner was truly the proverbial time capsule!

As divers worked to suck out the mud, others tackled the anchors. It was imperative to remove as much excess weight as possible prior to trying to lift her. The booms, masts, yardarms and gaffs also were raised.

When thcy were finally driven off the wreck by the icy blasts of winter much had been accomplished. With luck, in 1969 she could finally again see the light of day. Perhaps the most important accomplishment of 1968 was mental. The bunch of amateur divers that started the season had become far more professional and experienced, tempered by the hard work 19 fathoms down on the bottom of Lake Michigan. Amazing transformations can occur during 3,000 dives crawling in the muck of Lake Michigan.

Throughout the entire project money was a constant problem. No one had stepped forward to bankroll the operation so it was up to Hoffman to find the money to keep the salvage going. He did it by largely mortgaging everything he owned, bar, resort and home. While all the divers were dedicated to the success of the project, none came close to the commitment of Frank Hoffman.

When diving started again in the spring they returned to the job of sucking the thick and heavy mud out of her. When the mud was finally removed they used water pressure to jet six tunnels under the wreck, one for each of the heavy steel lifting cable needed to slowly carry her to the surface. Divers had to be especially careful as they cut the tunnels under the wreck the silt walls didn't collapse around them.

The scheme they worked out during the winter was simple in concept but as any work underwater, challenging to execute. A heavy lift barge loaned from Marinette Marine Corporation would be positioned directly over the wreck and using huge hand winches and steel lifting cables, the *Clark* would slowly be brought to a point just under the barge. The barge, with the schooner suspended beneath, would be towed to the nearby Marinette Marine yard where large shore-based cranes would finish the lift.

Some thought was given to using air bags or drums to lift the wreck. Attach enough of them to her, fill them with air and she would magically float to the surface. After careful consideration the crews realized it was far too dangerous. The bags or drums couldn't be controlled once inflated. If the balance was off only slightly the wreck would come up uneven, cables snap and she would plunge to the bottom with destruction following impact. If any of the lifting devices failed, the same asymmetric action would happen with the same deadly results. Should a drum break loose the air inside would launch it to the surface with enough force to destroy a boat or even kill a person. A barge with cables and winches was the safest method to use.

In July everything was in readiness for the lift. All they needed was perfect weather. Once started, they had to finish; there was no stopping halfway. Their weather window arrived and on July 22 the barge was positioned and cables attached. The next morning teams of six divers took turns cranking each winch. For every 100 turns the schooner rose a mere five inches! It was slow but steady and kept the strain on the old hull to the minimum. A man could barely last 100 turns but since this was the plan, the salvors stuck tenaciously to it. By 3:00 p.m. the wreck was within 60 feet of the surface when the crew received a radio report a storm was rapidly bearing down on the area. The barge crew immediately cut loose the four anchors holding the craft steady above the wreck and took it under tow for shore. If she sank again they wanted to make certain it was in shallow water. Meanwhile the winches continued to rotate to bring the wreck as high off the bottom as possible. There was some hope the squall would miss them but it had the salvors squarely in it's sight. For half an hour the salvors were buffeted by high winds and the sharp steep waves common to Green Bay before the squall blew itself out. No real damage was done. They continued to make their way to shallow water until the wreck found bottom in 45 feet. Anchoring the barge for the night, the exhausted men waited for the next day to finish the job.

The following morning a quick dive confirmed the cables were still properly placed. Cranking began again only stopping when the wreck was within inches of the barge's bottom. Her bowsprit projected clear of the water

The *Alvin Clark* had a retractable centerboard. This was a common feature on Great Lakes schooners and barks, allowing the crew to crank it up into the hull for entering shallow water ports and rivers, then down for stability on the open lake. The centerboard was down when she sank and try as they might, the divers couldn't get it back up into the hull. The only action was to leave it down and hope the water

Cranes at Marinette Marine raise the Alvin Clark *from the depths.*
Author

The Alvin Clark *shortly after breaking the surface from her long sojourn at the bottom of Green Bay. Note the wheel and related mechanism at the stern, very similar to that of the* Rouse Simmons. *Author*

was deep enough up the Menominee River to reach the Marinette Marine dock without destroying it.

On Friday July 25 the barge and suspended schooner were safe at Marinette Marine. Once the shore cranes were rigged to the cable and hauled away, the "Mystery Ship From Nineteen Fathoms" broke surface. It was 105 years and one month to the day after she sank!

Perhaps not daring to hope, the divers started to pump the water out of the schooner and after six hours she floated on her own bottom! Her old bilge pumps even worked! The caulking and seams were still tight.

Howard Chappelle, the dean of American maritime historians and senior historian of the Smithsonian Institution is quoted as telling Hoffman,"Your recovery of the schooner is of far greater importance than a few gold coins or hull fragment of a supposed treasure ship. In your find we will be now able to put together in great part, the real work-a-day craft of the past."

Problems started immediately she broke surface when her inexorable deterioration began.

Hoffman was later quoted as saying, "We took on the challenge of raising her, never knowing what we were getting into and what it would cost. Once we started on it we couldn't quit!"

Expenses piled up. Even though much of their equipment was cobbled up from junkyards and scrap piles, there were bills that had to be paid. Perhaps worse were the ones that could be but off, but only for a time. Eventually the devil would demand his due.

There seemed to be an attitude of "we raised it, now some-one else will take care of it. She is such a tremendous treas-ure the museum people will be falling over themselves to

The "Mystery Ship From 19-Fathoms."
Author

take care of it." This was extremely wishful thinking. Not a single institution, museum, deep pockets benefactor or municipality came forward to save the schooner. The State of Michigan didn't walk away from her, it ran, wanting nothing to do with the ship. The state's government historians were more interested in running old houses and rearranging artifacts in glass display cases, than getting their hands dirty with "real" history (in my humble opinion). Now I know some folks will turn apoplectic on reading this but unfortunately it was true. It is always easier to do what we always did than break the pattern.

Hoffman had only two absolute conditions for any savior; the schooner must be preserved and his expenses be reimbursed.

Salvaged wooden ships don't wait on hopes and dreams. The schooner was drying out and fast. After consulting with wood specialists the decision was made to built a plastic shed over the hull which was still at the Marinette Marine dock, and introduce live steam to keep the hull from drying out too fast. To a point the steaming was successful but certainly it was not the conservation methodology of choice. It's only real advantage was it was cheap.

The windlass was in remarkable condition. Author

The schooner would need a lot of "drying." Her hull planks were white oak, three inches thick and 70-feet long. The keel was a single piece of white oak over 100-feet long. It was common construction for the 1840s but that was a very long time ago. Finding white oak that large was now virtually impossible.

Eventually when the "drying out" was finished the schooner was moved to a special basin in Menominee, Michigan just across the river from Marinette and Hoffman tried to operate her as a tourist attraction to raise enough money to save her. The "Mystery Ship Seaport" was never a financial success. Menominee wasn't a tourist stop and Hoffman would need lots of folks visiting to help pay for her preservation. They never came.

As the years passed Hoffman slid deeper and deeper into debt and the schooner fell into greater decay. Winters in Menominee are harsh and the summer sun and winter freeze slowly tore the schooner apart. Water worked into the seams and on freezing, forced the seams open further and further. Pumps had to run continuously to keep her afloat and soon that wasn't enough; the basin was filled and the hull supported with dunnage.

While the *Alvin Clark*, the oldest merchant ship afloat, was slowly dying there were many other far less worthy ships being "saved." The State of Michigan was spending hundreds of thousands of dollars constructing a replica of the small sloop *Welcome* which would quickly rot out and require massive rebuilding. The Maritime Historical Society was trying to bring a second square-rigged ship as a companion to the one already at South Street Seaport Museum in New York (if one is good, two are better?), and the National Trust for Historic Preservation was preparing to distribute millions of dollars in grants to maritime museums including the National Maritime Museum in San Francisco (working to obtaining the rusted hulk of a square rigger in the Falkland Islands). The *Alvin Clark* didn't even appear on the radar screen. The shame of it is for five years or so after her salvage the *Alvin Clark* was easily the most authentic 19th century wooden ship in the country. The San Diego Maritime Museum's *Star Of India* previously billed as the oldest floating merchant ship (built in 1863) was now eclipsed by the *Alvin Clark* by 17 years!

Booty from the past. Author

The State of Michigan did recognize the schooner as a "Michigan Historical Site" in 1974 complete with the standard metal plaque. She was also added to the National Register of Historic Places and proclaimed a National Historical Treasure. Of course no money comes with the designations.

In 1981 the U.S. Coast Guard declared the *Alvin Clark* the oldest American documented commercial vessel in existence. The merchant vessel documentation division issued her number 3985, the oldest number they had available.

Certainly a very strong argument can be made that the schooner should have been left on the bottom. The cold water of Lake Michigan preserved it for this long so clearly it would have continued to do so for the foreseeable future. Bringing her to the surface was foolish unless a fully thought out and financed conservation plan was in place to handle her. In retrospect her ultimate destruction was certain from the beginning.

Saving the ship would have required a massive conservation effort, especially near constant application of Polyethylene Glycol (PEG). The compound has been used on many vessels in North America as well as Europe. The most famous application is probably the Swedish warship *Vasa*. It is expensive but very effective.

Both arguments are correct. But they also ignore the problem. It isn't whether she should be salvaged and under what conditions. She was salvaged, so the reality had to be dealt with not what should have been. Studying the *Alvin Clark* tragedy gives the clear impression the folks that could have saved her made a conscious decision not to do so. First, because they (official, certified, stamped and approved maritime archeologists) were not running the project but instead a gaggle of "amateur" scuba divers were, and second providing financial aid would have taken money away from their pet projects. The result was allowing her to fall into a pile of lumber. "That'll show 'em not to mess around with us professionals!"

References:

Avery, Thomas, *The Mystery Ship From Nineteen Fathoms* (Avery Color Studios, 1974), pp. 8-10, 18-20, 31-33, 40-41.

Bowen, Dana Thomas. "The Mystery Ship and it's Permanent Home," *Inland Seas*, Winter 1970, pp. 266-267.

62 ❊ Wood On The Bottom

Enrollment Documents, *Alvin Clark*, National Archives and Records Administration.

Green Bay Advocate, July 7, 1864.

History of the Great Lakes, Volume II (Cleveland: J.H. Beers and Company, 1899), pp. 732-734.

Lake Log Chips, May 30, 198; June 13, 1994.

McCutcheon, C.T., "The *Alvin Clark*, the Incredible Story of the Raising of a 19th Century Shipwreck," *Diving Times*, June-July 1983.

Manifest, Schooner *Alvin Clark*, October 20, November 2, 1846.

Donald G. May, M.D., "World's Oldest Floating Merchant Ship Beats the Depths But May Lose Race to Live With the Depths," *Sea History*, Spring, 1978.

May, "The World's Oldest Floating Merchant Ship Fights On," *Sea History*, Spring 1979.

May, "Survival Ahead for Merchant Ship," *Sea History*, Fall 1979.

Menominee Herald, October 7, 1969.

Milwaukee Sentinel, July 8, 1864.

The Mystery Ship From 19 Fathoms, Mystery Ship Seaport, Menominee, Michigan, n.d., pp. 1-5.

Polyethylene Glycol (PEG) - http://palimpsest.stanford.edu/byauth/grattan/peg.html.

Footnotes:

[1] See my book *Great Lakes Crime*, Avery Color Studios, 2004, pages 117-129 for a full discussion of lumber pirates of the Great Lakes.

[2] A cathead is a heavy timber projecting horizontally from the bow of a sailing ship through which the fall of the cat tackle is rove, the sheaves set in the cathead. This tackle heaves the ring of the anchor to the cathead a process called "catting the anchor."

[3] Deadeye - A round block of lignum vitae somewhat similar to the shell of a block. It has grooved holes through it and around the edge to secure the lower end of a shroud or chain plate.

[4] Bristol Fashion - Taken from the British port of Bristol; shipshape and seaman like, all correctly done.

PERSIAN

A Clear Weather Collision

Hauling Midwest grain from Chicago and Milwaukee to Lake Ontario ports, especially Buffalo and Oswego, was a common trade in the 1850s and 60s. Great fleets of fast schooners vied to be the first out in the spring and reach the elevators before their competitors. Large amounts of money was often wagered between crews, just to add a bit of spice to the trip. Some of the runs were incredibly fast. In 1854 the schooner *Canada* ran the 900 miles from Chicago to Buffalo in the lightning time of three days and eight hours, an average speed of 11.25 miles an hour! A more common time was between a week and ten days, but the old wind wagons were, of course, dependent on the vagaries of nature. No wind meant no-go. Too much wind meant sheltering in port or even heaving to on the open lake. The right amount of wind but in the wrong direction meant further frustration. Happiness was somewhere in between. Once the spring cargoes were finished they settled down to a more steady pace of back and forth runs. But danger still lurked behind every wave.

A case in point is the schooner *Persian*, typical of many of the schooners on the Great Lakes. Built in Oswego in 1855 the two master was 123-foot in length with a 22-foot beam and 345 gross tons. In 1868 she was neither old nor new, but rather in the prime of her working career.

After loading roughly a cargo of wheat in Milwaukee she made her way north on Lake Michigan using the slant of the wind to carry her to the Straits of Mackinac. She could have come up the north route,

The Bon Voyage. *She was a tinder box waiting to burn. Author*

passing Beaver Island well to the south or made the run though the Manitou Passage between the Manitou Islands and Michigan mainland.

Passing through the Straits she likely shaped her course down through the South Channel between Bois Blanc Island and the east shore of the mainland. The channel is roughly 18 miles long and a considerable shortcut to going around Bois Blanc Island (just south of Mackinac Island) before turning south on open Lake Huron. But as always it was the wind that played the tune she danced to.

Once beyond Cheboygan and Poe Reef she followed the coast down past broad Hammond Bay, really only a large bight or indentation in the shore than a fully-grown bay, and after a time the welcome sentinel of Forty Mile Point Light came into view.

It was here the schooner *E.B. Allen* came booming along and smashed hard into her starboard quarter! The collision was so sudden and unexpected all ten of the *Persian's* crew drowned in the resulting confusion. Some doubtless in the immediate confusion following the accident and others perhaps trapped below decks in the forecastle when she sank.

The collision rated a mention in Great Lakes newspapers but not much more. Shipwreck was as commonplace as automobile accidents are today so such passing interest really wasn't unusual. She was small, carried a common and easily replaceable cargo and the lost crew were only sailors, so it was no big thing. The *Persian* just faded away into history. The captain of the *Allen* was heavily censured in the press since conditions were ideal and she hit the *Persian* on her stern quarter thus making the collision impossible to explain away. Given fog, snow, night or storm, all conditions of bad visibility, a collision was understandable but clear weather?

Until July 26, 1991 when shipwreck searcher Ed Ellison found her with his sidescan sonar, the *Persian* was just a footnote in Great Lakes history. The long dead ship was sitting upright in 168 feet of Lake Huron. Her foremast still stood upright and soared to within 87 feet of the surface! She was, in the parlance of a wreck diver, a "virgin" shipwreck. No one else had found her or even worse, raped her of her artifacts.

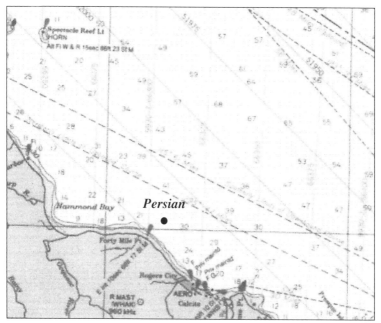

General location.

Compasses, dishes in stacks, cups and glasses on the cabin floor, all were powerful testimony no one visited her since her untimely death 123 years before. The deep hole cut by the *E.B. Allen's* bow still gaped open, a silent memorial to a terrible accident.

References:

Chips, November 25, 1991.

Detroit Free Press, October 2, 1868; November 28, 1991.

Ed Ellison, "Solving the Mystery of the *Persian*, Michigan History, July-August 1994, pp. 41-44.

Milwaukee Sentinel, October 2, 3, 1868.

Persian - Boatnerd.com

Persian - Stonehouse Collection

✳ **6**

INTO THE BREAKERS!

Shipwreck At Marquette

The men of the old U.S. Life-Saving Service played important roles in many Lake Superior shipwrecks. Time and again their big lifeboats and nimble surfboats proved the difference between life and death for sailors and passengers.

Starting in 1871 professionally manned Life-Saving Service stations began to be established nationally in areas of high concentrations of both shipwrecks and shipping. The first on the Great Lakes were operational in 1877. In was only fitting the first -stations on Lake Superior were placed along the infamous "Shipwreck Coast" in the eastern lake starting at Deer Park and including Two-Hearted River, Crisp's Point and Vermilion Point. The stations were about eight miles apart, which meant the night beach patrols marched four miles over the lonely beach before meeting another surfman coming from the next station. After exchanging a brass tag to prove they reached the halfway point the men turned around and made the long hike back to the home station. If they saw a shipwreck or found a victim in the wash of the waves, they burned a red Coston flare to alert both the shipwrecked crew and lookout in the station watchtower. A Life-Saving Service crew consisted of six to eight men called surfmen, with a keeper, often called the "captain" in charge. During the greater part of the Service's history the men were paid the munificent sum of 93 cents a day, out of which they had to pay for their rations and uniforms. There was no retirement, medical care or death gratuity or even guarantee of employment beyond the current season. They were hired only for the period of navigation on Great Lakes, normally mid-April - December 1. Next season they may or may not be hired again. Keepers were full-time and paid somewhat more, although not greatly so. Invariably the men came from maritime backgrounds - sailors or fishermen predominated. The Service wanted men expert in small boat handling and used to working in difficult conditions. No city slickers need apply.

Although the four original Lake Superior stations became operational in 1877, others were later added at Portage in 1887, Duluth 1895, Grand Marais 1900, Marquette 1891 and Eagle Harbor in 1914. All total, 61 stations were on the Great Lakes and 274 nationwide.[1] In January 1915 the Life-Saving Service combined with the old Revenue Marine to form today's Coast Guard.

Why a Life-Saving Station took so long to be established at Marquette is a bit of a mystery. There are no clear answers. The port was certainly busy enough. In the 1880s more traffic came and went than any other harbor on Lake Superior. And it wasn't only iron ore. Lumber, coal, passengers and general freight all added to the port's activity. The overriding reason may have been that Sumner I. Kimball, the General Superintendent of the Service didn't want to expand too quickly. It was important the stations he opened maintain the highest levels of professionalism. Good keepers, the men in charge of the stations, were hard to find so it was better he expanded at a controlled rate. Funding from Congress was always a year-to-year issue and if he placed incompetent crews in the field, all the fine work the others did could be swept aside in a single disaster. He was also under pressure from communities that wanted a station without regard to the actual need for one. And they had their political backers, members of Congress and Senators all pushing him to build a station in their home areas. Kimball needed all his considerable political skill to say no but still keep the congressmen smiling and the annual appropriations coming. Marquette was one of the communities pushing for a station but while there was plenty of shipping, where were the shipwrecks?

Into the Breakers - The *Wallaces*

The answer came at dawn on November 17, 1886. A terrible northeast gale was lashing the city. Blinding snow and sleet driven by a howling 50-miles per hour wind viciously assaulted folks brave enough to leave shelter. As the day grew older the gale increased in violence. Ships safely moored dockside cast off and anchored out in Iron Bay. Captains reluctant to leave the apparent safety of the docks had the decision made for them as mooring hawsers snapped like twine in the gusting wind.

The lake was churned to a witches' kettle of emotions. Enormous, furious waves poured over the breakwater in cold gray sheets of terror. Superior resembled a sea of gray-flaked bubbling foam. At 2:00 p.m. a huge wave cascaded over the light tower at the end of the breakwater completely tearing the wooden structure off its foundations and tumbling it into the lake. The large rolling mill dock was literally submerged by the high waves and a veritable mountain of lumber, shingles and lath piled on it for shipment was swept into the harbor.

During the two days of the worst of the gale 30 vessels on the lake wrecked, over a million dollars in property lost and the lives of 40 sailors forfeited. Superior was certainly on a rampage!

The Lower Harbor breakwater light was washed off by a huge wave, ending up on the beach. Author

Later in the afternoon the hardy crowds that ventured outside to watch the terrible ravages of the gale were treated to the rare sight of a lone schooner running close reefed through the gale-whipped lake

The wrecked Florida. *Author*

and dead for the rocky breakwater. If she hit, it was certain death for ship and crew. Without waiting for a signal Captain John Frink of the tug *Gillett* steamed out through the breaking seas, put a towing hawser aboard her and handily dragged her into safe harbor. She turned out to be the *Eliza Gerlach* and with the prevailing gale, Frink's feat was a masterwork of seamanship but considering what was yet to come, just prelude.

Minutes after the *Gillett* cast off the *Gerlach*, the steamer *Iron Chief* frantically signaled she sighted another schooner further out and she was in evident distress!

The schooner, later identified as the *Florida*, entered the outer harbor in a dense snow squall solely by using her hand-powered foghorn. She was in effect navigating by listening for the echo off the nearby land as well as replies from anchored ships. But in the general confusion she ran too close to the beach and unable to come about, dropped her anchors and prayed they would hold. They didn't and the blasts of wind bounced the flukes over the bottom like plows in a concrete parking lot! It would only be a short time before she crashed into the rocks off the Whetstone Creek in South Marquette.

After throwing a few more bags of coal aboard to feed his voracious boiler fire, Frink brought the snub bow of the *Gillett* around and steamed across the churning harbor to the area indicated by the *Iron Chief*. Within minutes the *Florida* loomed out of the snow and Frink smartly backed down under her stern quarter yelling for the crew to jump to his deck. With both vessels bobbling wildly in the surging lake and the schooner deck being swept by an occasional wave, it was no easy matter. One by one the eight men aboard the *Florida* made the jump to the tug except for one. The lone casualty happened when the mate hesitated at the critical moment, fell into the water and was crushed to death when the two ships surged together.

The intrepid Captain Frink brought the *Gillett* with the shaken *Florida* crewmen back to the Merchandise Dock. Frink's actions in getting the men off the schooner likely saved their lives as she later broke in two after striking the rocks.

The *Mining Journal* commented on the rescue saying, "If ever a man deserved the government's lifesaving medal... John Frink is the man!" Frink didn't receive a medal. Whether one was applied for and

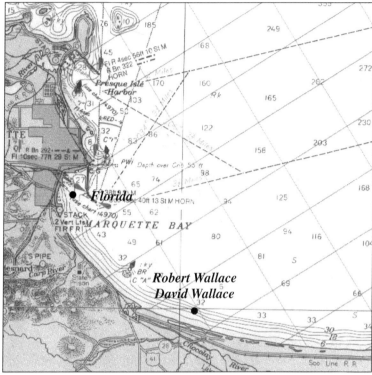

General locations.

denied or never requested is unknown. It isn't unlikely the paper was simply "blowing smoke" either.

Throughout the night of the 17th the dreadful storm continued to grow in demonic fury. When the utter blackness of night gave way grudgingly to the cold gray of dawn two more casualties were discovered. The steamer *Robert Wallace* and her tow, the schooner-barge *David Wallace*, were aground off the Chocolay River. The forlorn blasts of the steamer's whistle finally attracted someone's attention. Both ships were stern on with the schooner being nearest the beach. Immediate reports said the schooner was broken in two places with her after cabin gone, a total loss! Observers said waves were regularly washing over both ships. When the cold water washed down the steamer's companionway and on to the boiler huge clouds of steam billowed into the air. She had settled so deep her decks were nearly level with the water.

Clearly something had to be done to save the crews. Before the end of the morning local citizens sent a yawl by wagon to the beach opposite the wrecks. Manned by five volunteers from the various ships in the harbor including men from the *Florida*, the yawl made several efforts to reach the *Wallaces*. Each time she was forced back by the seas. The yawl wasn't trying to take the crew of the wrecks off as such but rather drag a rope out the sailors could use to make their own way to shore. Even if such a rope was run the likelihood of the men being able to successfully reach safety was very low.

In the gathering gloom five huge bonfires built and fed by anxious townspeople cast an unearthly glow over the beach. The dancing flames at least let the sailors know help was at hand and also gave light and warmth to the would-be rescuers. Refusing to give up, an old and very heavy iron mortar was sent for from the Marquette Powder Works on the Dead River several miles distant with the intention of firing a line to the wrecks. Since the touchhole had been spiked to prevent its use, the hole had to be drilled out and relined occasioning more delay. Doubtless the mortar was spiked because it was unsafe to fire, precisely what the would-be rescuers wanted to do with it. Just before dark a wagon delivered it to the beach. Under the direction of James Freeman, who in theory knew what he was doing, the black iron monster was loaded with a charge of black powder. A 24-pound shot with a line fastened to it was rammed home.

When things looked right, Freeman lit the fuse, the old mortar boomed and line shot out a bare 50 feet before falling into the lake. Quickly the line was coiled again and mortar recharged but now with a much larger quantity of black powder. The weighty ball was again loaded and a new fuse pushed down the touchhole. A burning stick from a bonfire lit the fuse and for a second it sputtered then the old mortar roared but instead of throwing the ball and line toward the wreck, it burst, sending deadly iron fragments whistling past would-be rescuers ringing ears! Luckily no one was injured.

The sailors on the wrecks weren't waiting for help from shore. They knew there was no Life-Saving Service Station in Marquette and by now had no confidence in the townsfolk to save them. The sailors tried

In this photo taken the day after the storm, the schooner-barge David Wallace *is on the left and steamer* Robert Wallace *on the right. Author*

to float ropes ashore tied to pieces of wreckage. Each attempt failed though not as spectacularly as the bursting mortar! The tug *Jay C. Morse* tried to reach the steamer from the lake side but was driven away by the crashing seas.

One person in the crowd kept his wits about him, knowing the local folks amateurish efforts were doomed to failure. Captain Frink took action, telegraphing the Life-Saving Station at Portage Entry, on the north entrance to the Keweenaw Ship Canal for assistance. The nearest telegraph office was in Houghton, 15 miles distant, so the message was delivered to Keeper Albert Ocha by the captain of the tug *James W. Croze.* Running down the ship canal to the station. (See inset page 115.)

It was 4:00 p.m. and darkness fast approaching when Ocha received the telegram and he wasted no time. Alerting the Marquette, Houghton and Ontonagon Railroad in Houghton to get a special train ready for the run to Marquette, he assembled his crew, launched his big lifeboat and loaded his beach apparatus and surfmen aboard the *Croze.* When all was ready the tug, towing the lifeboat behind, returned to Houghton at full speed steaming down the canal in a swirling blizzard of snow. A wheezing locomotive with two flatcars and coach stood by waiting

Lifeboat launching at the Portage Life-Saving Service Station.
Michigan Technological University Archives

their arrival. The same storm that was lashing Marquette was attacking the Keweenaw too! Powerful wind blasts shook trees and a blizzard covered the world in a desperate swirl of white.

Ocha was one of the legendary keepers of the Service. Utterly fearless, he led his men in many courageous rescues. After wrestling the heavy lifeboat onto a flatcar and bracing it up properly and loading the beach apparatus on the second flatcar, Ocha and his surfmen climbed into the coach and at 7:45 p.m. signaled they were ready. After a loud whistle blast to clear the way, Engineer Henry Jackson rammed the throttle of engine 39 to the firewall and the big drive wheels threw a shower of sparks as they clawed for traction on the snow covered rails. Literally blowing through huge snowdrifts blocking the tracks, the special train flew for Marquette at times reaching 60 miles an hour! Engineer Jackson was known by some local folk as a daredevil - a Keweenaw version of the mythical Casey Jones. But on this desperate night he was the perfect man for the job. Every minute lost could mean lost lives and Henry Jackson wasn't going to lose any minutes on his run!

Ocha had the engineer stop briefly at the Michigamme station about half way to Marquette to telegraph ahead to Frink asking him to have wagons ready to take the lifeboat and other gear to the wreck site and to lay in a good supply of storm lanterns and oil.

The special arrived at the Marquette station at 10:55 p.m. after a fast three hour and ten minute run, a new record for the railroad line. The 110-mile dash through the blizzard became part of Life-Saving Service legend celebrated in story and poem. Townsfolk waiting at the station recalled when the snow encased train puffed into the station it appeared like a ghostly apparition.

At Marquette the life-savers transferred to a waiting second special train provided by the Detroit, Mackinac and Marquette Railway to take them a few miles closer to the Chocolay. As at Houghton, local volunteers helped transfer the lifeboat and beach apparatus. Captain Frink was standing by in Chocolay with several wagons and sleighs and a crew of men to help load and transport the lifeboat and other equipment from the train to the beach opposite the wreck. Much of the trip was made over a hastily laid corduroy road of driftwood leading down to the water's edge but it was still hard going. Frink also had a cache of food donated by local merchants to fuel life-savers and shipwreck victims alike.

Barreling through the night, a "special" bringing the Portage Life-Savers to Marquette blasted through a blizzard to reach the city. Author

Life-Saving crew hauling a beach apparatus cart. Author

The crowd at Chocolay beach had been gathering since 1:00 p.m. and by the time Ocha and his men arrived it numbered over 400 people. The large throng was eager to help and they quickly hauled all of the life-saving equipment, including the lifeboat to the beach. Remember, Ocha had never seen either wreck. He was only working with what he was told and what little he could see from the flash of breaking waves on the near invisible hulls. It was at best a very confusing situation.

Shortly after midnight Ocha tried to fire a line to the steamer with his Lyle gun but it was extremely difficult to do in the dark. Lyle gun range is only about 400 yards and unable to make out the distance, he could have fired short. He also could have dropped the line directly across the deck but in the storm and darkness the thin line was unseen or the sailors too afraid to venture out on the wave-washed deck to get it.

About 2:00 a.m. Ocha decided to try the lifeboat but the energetic crowd proved more hindrance than help. Their brute strength was important to carry the heavy lifeboat into the water for launching but apparently in pushing it away, some folks damaged the rudder, bending an iron strapping and splitting the wood. Regardless, Ocha and his crew continued on into the icy darkness. With a damaged rudder Ocha was unable to control the lifeboat as expertly as he should and by the time the lifeboat reached the third bar it had filled three times with water. The damaged boat couldn't continue on and Ocha reluctantly brought her back to shore. While part of his crew was set to repairing the rudder by the dull yellow glow of an oil lantern, Ocha tried again with the Lyle gun. Again the shot either failed to reach the wrecks or the line went unseen.

By daybreak the lifeboat was hastily repaired and again ready to launch. This time the crowd followed the keepers instructions to the letter and the lifeboat launched without damage. Frantically the surfmen pulled for the steamer, now clearly visible, through the storm. Breaking seas continuously inundated the lifeboat but still she kept on, heading unfailingly for the steamer *Robert Wallace*. Breaking waves tumbled into the lifeboat and some men bailed while others bent hard at the oars. The lifeboat crested wave after wave only to drop from sight in the following trough. It was a heart stopping show to the folks safe ashore. After reaching the lee of the steamer, and protected from the worst of the seas, Ocha gave the order and nine of the steamers' crew leaped into the wildly tossing lifeboat. The steamer looked like a shell of ice. The lifeboat was soon equally coated.

The surfmen quickly brought the sailors to shore and went out twice more fighting their way over the treacherous bar before removing another six men from the steamer and nine from the *David Wallace*. On the last trip out the rudder split again but Ocha steered by directing his men at the oars "throttling" back one side and increasing the other. It was a maneuver only a highly trained crew and very skilled keeper could pull off. By 9:30 a.m. all were safe on the beach, a fine example of the efficiency and ability of a professional Life-Saving Service crew.

Wagons provided by Captain Frink took the bedraggled survivors to Marquette's European Hotel. The sailors hadn't eaten in 36 hours and not only were wet and cold, but ravenous too! By contrast the ice covered Life-Savers had to make do with hot coffee and food while standing by the flickering bonfires. They still had to repair the lifeboat, get her and all their gear back on the wagons, up the rough corduroy trail, on the railcars and eventually back to Portage arriving about 1:00 p.m. the following day.

The pure endurance of the life-savers was incredible. When originally alerted by the telegram from Frink at 4:00 p.m. they had

The steamer Robert Wallace. *Author*

been working as normal since 6:00 a.m. Then followed the effort of moving the lifeboat and equipment to Houghton, loading it, a three hour and ten minute dash through a blizzard at rocket-like speeds, transferring the gear in Marquette and yet again at Chocolay to get it to the beach, setting up the beach apparatus for the Lyle gun attempt, making the rescue effort in the lifeboat, beaching and repairing it, trying the Lyle gun again, launching the lifeboat a second time and making three desperate trips to the wrecks to remove the crew and most of the effort being accomplished in the midst of a screaming gale. At no point in this litany of labor was there a chance for any substantial rest. Certainly dozing off in the train while a wild-eyed Henry Jackson firewalled them to Marquette was not "restful." These brave men must have been well done in by the time the last sailor came ashore. And remember, they still had to retrace all steps to return quickly to their station in Portage Entry to be ready for another call to action!

Interviewed later Captain Henry Wallace of the *David Wallace* and Captain Frank H. Brown of the *Robert Wallace* said they left Duluth for Buffalo at 4:00 p.m. on Monday in fair weather. By Wednesday they were overtaken by a heavy gale 45 miles West of Stannard's Rock. With the blinding snow reducing visibility to near zero, they decided to run before the gale. By midnight the *Robert Wallace* had throttled back her engine and was proceeding carefully since her location wasn't known. At 1:00 p.m. on Thursday the steamer went hard aground about 1,000 feet offshore, the schooner sheering around and striking closer to the beach. Both vessels slewed around with their bows facing seaward an orientation, which greatly lessened damage from the huge combers. Regardless great waves began to batter both ships and the crews sheltered in the forecastles.

Brown, 54 years of age, spent 35 years sailing the lakes, the last 25 as a captain. This was his first shipwreck. He later said, "The driving snow and sleet made it impossible to see a rod ahead. Owing to the tremendous sea, soundings were impossible and we had no means of ascertaining our position... We had no idea we were near land, so far out of our reckoning were we. I supposed we were off Michipicoten (Island)." Doubtless the missing breakwater light, washed off by the waves earlier in the storm may have played a role too.

Both vessels were owned by David Wallace and Company of Lorain, Ohio and nearly new. The steamer, built by Radcliffe of Cleveland in 1882, rated at A-1 at 1,189 gross tons. The schooner, built the year before was 216 feet in length and 1,050 gross tons. The *Robert Wallace* carried 49,000 bushels of grain and *David Wallace* 55,000. The wheat in both ships was valued at $100,000. In addition, the steamer's value was placed at $80,000 and schooner $50,000.

When both captains and crews were told the Life-Savers were brought down from Portage via a special train they were amazed! The sailors couldn't believe railroad men could be so public spirited.

When the gale moderated the following day both captains went out to their boats and gave them a complete examination. After removing valuables they telegraphed for salvage tugs hoping to be able to pull them off the beach quickly.

Both ships were well known in Marquette, frequently calling to load ore. When they made their maiden call in June, 1884, the *David Wallace* was called a "splendid four master" and it was commented she flew a Blaine and Logan flag from her mainmast. It was common practice for ship owners to advertise their candidates for political office in this manner. James G. Blaine of Maine was running for President and John Logan for Vice President on the Republican ticket in the 1884 election.

The *Robert Wallace's* Marquette trials weren't over. On November 21 heavy black smoke was seen curling up from her decks. It seems some of her crew were aboard getting ready for expected salvage pumps and had a fire going in a coal stove in the hallway forward. The men had some clothing hanging nearby to dry. When noontime rolled around they went over to the *David Wallace* for lunch leaving the fire unattended. Apparently some of the clothing overheated, and caught fire, spreading rapidly to the wooden structure. Crewmen tried to extinguish it but it was too far along. Only the the timely arrival of Captain Brown and the tug *Gillett* with her fire monitor saved the ship from complete destruction, but damage was major including her entire forward deck cabin.

Six days after the fire wreckers had the steamer floating free and in Marquette harbor. Her bottom was considerably damaged and she floated so low when the tugs *Champion* and *J.C. Adams* brought her in, she grounded 200 feet short of the Merchandise Dock. A crew of local laborers soon emptied her wheat cargo by pick and shovel and steam pump. When wheat gets wet it swells and in the case of the steamer, it forces the lower deck out of shape and expanded through the resulting gaps into the boiler and engine rooms completely filling both spaces. The grain packed so tight, picks were needed to break it loose. About 30,000 bushels of undamaged wheat was sent by railroad boxcar to Milwaukee. The water soaked wheat was dumped in the harbor spewed out by several large steam pumps leaving a creamy foam across the surface.

The *David Wallace* remained fast on the sand bar until 5:00 p.m. on December 10 when the combined efforts of the tugs *Adams* and *Gillett* finally pulled her free. Two hours later she was safely in the harbor where day laborers unloaded her wheat too. She lost all but 18,000 bushels of her cargo. Although both ships were floating in the harbor, salvage costs were considerable, reaching $30,000.

The pair remained in Marquette over the winter. In the spring Captain Brown arrived with a crew and after some days working on them, arranged to have the pair towed to Detroit for complete repair. It was later announced the steamer cost $20,000 to be repaired and the schooner, $7,580.

The *Robert Wallace* remained in service until November 17, 1902 when she foundered in a gale southeast of Two-Harbors, Minnesota. It was 16 years to the day after her Marquette adventure. Her crew was saved by the steamer *Ashland*. The *David Wallace* met her end in August, 1915 sinking off Matinecus Rock off the Maine coast. It was a very long way from the beach in Marquette.

References:

Annual Report, US Life-Saving Service - 1887.

Beeson's Directory 1902, p. 172.

Daily Mining Journal, November 30, 1963.

Journal of the Life-Saving Station at Portage Entry, November 1886, RG26 NARA.

Journal of the Lighthouse Station at Marquette, November - December 1886, RG26, NARA.

Mining Journal, November 20, 27, December 4, 11, 1886, May 28, July 2, 1887.

William D. O'Connor, *Heroes of the Storm* (Houghton, Mifflin and Company: New York, 1904), pp. 269-281.

"Remembering Other Novembers," *The Nor'Easter, Journal of the Lake Superior Marine Museum Association*, September - October 1986, pp 1-3.

Robert Wallace - www.boatnerd.com

Wallaces File - Stonehouse Collection.

Into the Breakers - Three More Wrecks

Less than a year after the *Wallaces* and *Florida* wrecks, another gale of equal intensity played havoc with Marquette area shipping. The blow began with a tearing 40 plus mile per hour wind coming dead from the east; quickly it boxed the compass until it was screaming out of the northwest. Increasing in velocity it made a final shift to the north and began to pile up a terrific sea. As with the great gale of the previous year, the lure of watching nature's destructive fury brought hundreds of city residents out of the comfort of their homes. From vantage places like Lighthouse Point, they were treated to the spectacle of huge greybeards smashing into the breakwater sending clouds of spray high into the air. All the while violent snow squalls swept across the lake alternately blinding the watchers with a cloud of swirling nothing then passing.

In the late evening of October 23 word reached the city the schooner *George Sherman* wrecked on Shot Point, eight miles to the east. Considering the raging storm, it came as no surprise.

Captain Nelson Gifford of the *Sherman* explained later how she ended up on the rocks. He said he hauled past the Soo at 7:00 a.m. Saturday, October 22, and all went well until that night when he struck

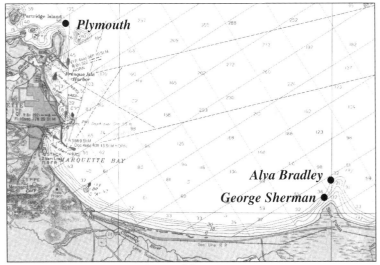

General locations.

a storm off Whitefish Point. By 7:00 a.m. the next day heavy swirls of crystalline snow reduced visibility to less than a boat's length and blinded the lookout. Previously, the schooner picked up the schooner *Alva Bradley* and, as both captains were friends, sailed in company until the snow separated them. Captain Gifford realized the north wind had pushed him too close to shore and tried to haul off but his efforts were rewarded by the heavy scraping of his hull on the rocks. The *Sherman* was hard aground!

Quickly assessing his ship was stuck fast, he decided to get his crew ashore as soon as possible. Within minutes the yawl was over the side and crew pulling for the beach. As if in a last desperate attempt to destroy them, the schooner's mainmast toppled and fell into the lake, narrowly missing the bobbing yawl.

The wet, cold and bedraggled survivors stumbled ashore on the rocky Shot Point beach at 3:30 p.m. For the next two and a half hours the stunned crew wandered through the dense woods utterly lost. At 6:00 p.m. they stumbled across a set of railroad tracks just in time to flag down an approaching train. Given a ride to town, they reported the wreck.

None of the crew of the *Sherman* was lost or injured. However all were bone tired and suffering from exhaustion, especially the female cook who had to be carried during the last part of the wandering.

Built in Cleveland by Quayle and Martin in 1862, she was rebuilt in 1878, 1880 and 1884. Rated B-1, she was 307 registered tons and 140 feet long. Owned by William Cunningham of Cleveland, she carried coal consigned to the Pickands Mather Company in Marquette. Captain Gifford claimed the *Sherman* was his first wreck in 49 years of sailing, a remarkable record in an age when shipwreck was commonplace.

Shortly after the news of the *Sherman* reached town word of another wrecked schooner, the *Alva Bradley*, was on the street. When the snow squalls finally ceased the beleaguered schooner could be plainly seen from the city. Laying further out than the *Sherman*, huge waves were breaking 20 feet over her decks. By 10:00 p.m. Sunday Marquette's Marshall Ryan led a search party to the site hoping to find the crew wandering in the woods as the *Sherman's* crew did. They found nothing. Where was the crew?

———————

First light Monday revealed the crew still hunkered down aboard the schooner. In an attempted rescue, the tug *Adams* came over from the city but the heavy seas kept her from coming any closer than a half mile. The unrelenting seas continued to wash over the *Bradley*. The breakers also wreaked havoc with the *Sherman* as Captain Gifford discovered when he returned to the site about the same time as the *Adams* made her abortive approach. The schooner's stern appeared to be completely gone and the hull badly broken.

Learning from the *Wallaces* of the year before, the townspeople didn't waste their time with tries at amateur rescue, instead immediately telegraphing Keeper Ocha at Portage for his crew. The Life-Savers repeated the same drill as before, although Henry Jackson didn't have to blast his way through the piling drifts to reach Marquette. In another change Ocha brought his smaller and lighter surfboat instead of big lifeboat. Doubtless he remembered the difficulty in moving the big boat from train to beach the previous year.

Folks kept huge bonfires burning at the beach opposite the *Bradley* letting the survivors know help was coming. Others stood by at the train station with wagons ready to help transfer the surfboat and beach apparatus.

The schooner-barge Plymouth *aground at Presque Isle. Author*

Meanwhile there was a third wreck, the schooner *Plymouth*. Besides revealing the *Bradley* off Shot Point, the thin gray dawn showed the steamer *Hurlburt* riding at anchor in harbor. Her captain hurriedly reported he lost his tow, the *Plymouth*, on Presque Isle during the night's storm.

Acting on the captain's report, the tug *Adams* battled through the waves to arrive off the area called Sunset Point on the northwest side of the island where she found the *Plymouth* hard on the rocks and crew still aboard. The seas were rolling too high for the tug to lay up to the schooner and prevented the schooner's crew from reaching shore in the yawl but they were safe aboard for the time being so there was no hurry to get them off.

Both *Hurlburt* and *Plymouth* were heavily laden with coal and bound for Ashland when slammed by the storm. The powerful winds forced the pair south of their intended course and directly into Presque Isle. When the cliffs of the island loomed up directly in front of the steamer's captain, he frantically turned hard to starboard and trying to claw out into the open lake but the strain of the turn and cumulative wearing away by the gale broke the towing hawser and the *Plymouth* crashed hard into the rocks.

The *Plymouth* was originally built as a propeller in Cleveland in 1854 by the Lafrinier Yard. Owned by Crosthwaite of Buffalo, she was 876 gross registered tons and converted into a schooner-barge in 1884.

The Life-Saving crew from Portage arrived in Marquette at 10:00 p.m. but instead of changing rail lines to Chocolay as he did the previous year, Ocha had the flatcar with the surfboat run through the switchyard and out on to the Merchandise Dock where the boat was craned into the water. Ocha was taking no chances with over zealous volunteers damaging his surfboat.

Once the Life-Savers were aboard the surfboat and Ocha signaled he was ready, the *Adams* passed a towline and headed for the wreck. Getting a tow rather than rowing saved the Life-Savers' strength and was a faster way to travel the eight miles to the wreck but it was still a rough and wet trip with freezing spray drenching the men every time the boat shouldered into a cresting wave. *Adams* and her tow drove on through the black and storm-striven night. About a mile and a half seaward of the *Bradley* the tug dropped the tow and Ocha barked out

the command, "out oars, pull together" and swinging his sweep oar
hard a starboard, brought the surfboat around for the wreck. At 2:00
a.m. she reached her destination, the protected lee of the schooner.

Even though the night was blacker than sin, the sailors on the
Bradley had strained to see the approaching tug and later wildly
plunging lifeboat trailing along behind. Other than the bonfires the
only real illumination came from occasional bursts of sparks spewing
from the tug's stack. But they knew rescue was close at hand.

As soon as Ocha gave his approval Captain A.B. Parsons and his
ten man crew tumbled into the surfboat and safety. Clearing the wreck
the life-savers pulled for the spot the *Adams* should have hove to after
dropping the surfboat. That was the plan. The tug was to wait for them
and provide a tow back to the harbor. But regardless of how hard he
looked, Ocha couldn't see the tug and reluctantly concluded she
wasn't there. Did she abandon them or founder in the cresting seas?
Ocha wanted to make the long pull back to Marquette but glancing at
the nearly frozen schooner's crew huddled in the bottom of the boat he
knew some of them wouldn't make it. Reluctantly he brought the
surfboat back to the lee of the *Bradley* where all rested for a short
period. Since the bonfires were still burning furiously on the nearby
beach and hot drinks, food and blankets so close, he brought the
surfboat onto the beach. Doubtless a bottle or two of strong stimulants
was on hand to keep the heart going too!

The survivors were bundled off to Marquette but Ocha and his men
waited by the fires until daybreak when they pushed the surfboat back
into the breakers and rowed out to the *Adams*, which had returned to
the rendezvous position offshore. After what were likely some very
choice words by Ocha with the tug's captain, the Life-Savers were
towed back to the Merchandise Dock arriving at 9:00 a.m. When they
reached the dock the Life-Savers were actually frozen to the thwarts
by the thick ice. The tug's captain later claimed he understood he was
supposed to return at daybreak as he did, not wait for Ocha's return
that night.

Questioned later the schooner's crew said they struck the rocks
soon after the *Sherman* and thought they were surely lost when the
Sherman began to break-up. The *Bradley* appeared to be pounding
heavily too and the crew thought it only a matter of time before she

completely went to pieces. The decks quickly hogged and she appeared broken between the mainmast and centerboard hatch.[2]

Like the *Sherman* the *Bradley* was built in Cleveland by Quayle and Martin in 1870, repaired in 1882 and in 1883. She was registered at 934 gross tons and measured 192 feet overall. Her cargo of coal was consigned to the South Shore Railroad.

As in 1886 the hero of the day was Keeper Albert Ocha. Described by the *Mining Journal* as "an old hand at the business though young in years... quiet, cool and daring and the splendid manner in which he managed his boat and its living freight in the intense darkness and heavy sea Monday night is warmly commented on by the members of the *Bradley* crew." He was still angry for some time after the rescue concerning the behavior of the *Adams*. Ocha was heard to state, "If the schooner's crew could have stood it, I would have pulled into Marquette harbor and moored alongside the *Adams*."

To put it all in proper perspective, the two rescues Ocha led from Portage to Marquette were the longest overland rescues in the 44-year history of the Life-Saving Service! Certainly they added to his status of one of the most indomitable keepers on the Great Lakes.

Meanwhile, at the *Plymouth*, the crew remained with the vessel until late evening when Captain Rivard and two of his crew successfully reached shore in the schooner-barge's yawl. Soon after they landed the lake noticeably calmed and the remainder of the crew followed.

When the lake calmed, salvage operations were immediately started on all three ships. On October 28 the tug *Gillett* began lightering the coal from the *Bradley* and pumping out her flooded hold. The quick work almost released the schooner but before the tug was able to free her, the wind shifted northwest and by 5:00 p.m. was blowing at gale force driving the salvors off the wreck.

The *Plymouth* looked far worse and within days the owners abandoned her to the underwriters. Better they take the money and run than deal with an old schooner-barge on the rocks! When the weather finally moderated the wreckers were back on her but without achieving any real success. Another sudden northwest gale forced them off her during the first week of November, badly damaging two of their lighters when it blew them on the rocky shore opposite the wreck. After salvaging his own losses the wrecker, Captain C. Hebard of Pequaming, took his gear and went home, declaring the *Plymouth* a complete loss. Apparently Hebard wasn't able to recover much of the coal. Captains Rivard and Quinn representing the underwriters agreed, officially declaring her a total loss on November 8.

Other marine men weren't so certain about the "total" loss. On November 26, J. H. Gillett of Marquette, the salvor of the *Wallaces,* purchased the cargo of coal from Peter White, the local agent for the Boston Marine Insurance Company for a paltry $200. It wasn't often old Peter, one of the founders of Marquette and a very astute businessman, came out second best in a deal but this was one time he certainly did. Gillett was willing to gamble the *Plymouth* would stay together long enough to remove the majority of the 1,300 tons of coal. Apparently Gillett had second thoughts because a week later he sold the coal to Peter Munson and Company for $650 taking a quick and clear profit of $450. Munson in turn contracted to deliver the coal to Pickands Mather Company at $3.25 a ton. He needed just 200 tons to, in theory, break even. Instead of rushing out to the wreck Munson

Salvaging the Plymouth's *coal cargo during winter. Author*

bided his time and when the lake froze over, used horses, sleighs and chutes to unload the coal and haul it to the buyer.

Another gambler was Mayor Hull from St. Ignace. He purchased the hull for a mere $1,200. If she survived the winter and he could get her off the rocks, the hull could be worth upwards of $20,000. The local folks thought he made a bad deal, only buying a pile of soon-to-be kindling.

In May of 1888 the big Reid wrecking tug *Mockingbird* battered her way through the rotten spring ice to be the first vessel into Marquette. Quickly recoaling, she headed for the *Plymouth* anxious to start work. After the hard hat diver from the tug took a long look at the hull he pronounced her in "good shape." The crew worked on the wreck for the next six weeks occasionally being driven off by northwest seas but always returning to the job.

The *Plymouth* and the work of the wreckers became a tourist attraction for local folks. The city recently acquired Presque Isle from the federal government for use as a park and a new road around the perimeter provided access right up to the wreck site. There were even organized weekend picnic outings to see the wreck.

On June 23 three more Reid tugs arrived each carrying part of a cargo of 13,000 empty barrels. The crew from the *Mockingbird* already placed 12,000 in the *Plymouth's* hold and their combined buoyancy nearly floated her free. By early September the rest of the barrels were in position and the *Plymouth* came off the rocks.[3] Not wasting time one of the tugs passed a hawser to her and it was off to St. Ignace for thorough repair at the company yard. Again the Reid company succeeded where other, less imaginative and tenacious salvagers failed.

The *Plymouth* remained in service until foundering with all seven hands off Garden Island in northern Lake Michigan in the great storm of November 1913. She was under tow of the tug *James H. Martin* who abandoned her in the lee of the island when the worst of the storm roared down on the them. Left to her fate, the *Plymouth* simply disappeared. A note in a bottle reportedly from one of the men aboard her complained the *Martin* "left us and never even said good-bye."

When Reid was busy with the *Plymouth* he was also working on the wreck of the *Arizona*. The 189-foot wooden steamer had sheltered in

Marquette during the early hours of November 17, 1887. When the lake moderated in the afternoon she headed out to continue her trip to Houghton and later Duluth. Deep in her holds was a cargo of mining machinery, barreled cement, boxes of candles, a batch of mixed acids and a large quantity of oil. It was the last two items that would get her into deep trouble.

When she struck a northwest squall off Big Bay a barrel of acid spilled and the seething liquid in turn ignited the wooden deck, which set fire to the candles and oil, eventually setting the entire ship ablaze. The acid fumes also drove every one on deck for breathable air. Before fleeing the engineroom the chief engineer had his crew stoke the boilers as high as possible, deciding wherever the *Arizona* was going she needed power. Captain Glazer decided returning to Marquette was the best thing for his ship and crew (although not for the city).

As she charged toward the city huge clouds of bright orange smoke, the result of the burning acid, billowed out behind her. She must have been a strange sight, ablaze with fire, orange smoke pouring from her and still roaring full tilt through the cresting seas! Rounding the breakwater the captain blew frantic blasts with his whistle warning everyone clear of his charging ship. Folks ashore saw the seagoing conflagration coming and fire bells summoned the city fire department

The steamer Arizona *ablaze at the breakwater. Note the tug putting a stream of water into the burning ship, stack of the city waterworks and wood catwalk above the breakwater. Author*

The burned out Arizona. *Note the huge piles of lumber on the docks behind her. Had the lumber caught fire the whole city might have gone up in a blaze of glory. Author*

to stand ready for action. Once in the harbor Captain Glazer turned hard to starboard and put her bow directly into the rock breakwater, hitting so hard the impact point of the breakwater was knocked a foot out of true! The crew quickly jumped to the rocks and safety. But the *Arizona's* propeller was still turning and it pushed the ship to port and she scraped along the rocks, literally chasing the crew as they fled to shore. The steamer finally grounded in shallow water and burned to the water's edge. The Marquette Fire Department soon arrived on scene but their steam pumps were too little, too late to extinguish the blaze. The ship burned for 24 hours and for a time, it was feared the entire city would catch fire from the huge showers of sparks.

Like the *Plymouth*, the *Arizona* was also considered a total loss. Perhaps thinking he had little to lose, Reid also purchased the steamer for a pittance of her former value. When she burned the *Arizona*, built in Cleveland in 1865, was worth $90,000. The ever tenacious Reid succeeded in salvaging her and rebuilt her as a bulk freighter. She ran until 1922 when she burned in the St. Lawrence River near St. Vincent, New York, a total loss.

Why the *Plymouth* survived her rocky ordeal is an open question. By all rights the schooner should have gone to pieces. But remember, she was built as a propeller, or more correctly a wooden package

The Arizona *after rebuilding. Author*

freight steamer, which meant her hull was stronger than a schooner's. Reid knew this fact and likely factored it into his decision to gamble on her survival.

Getting the *Bradley* off was far easier than the *Plymouth*. The Gillett Company quickly went to work on her and by November 2 had her afloat. With the steamer *S.E. Sheldon* towing and the *Gillett* and *Adams*

The small harbor tug A.C. Adams *helped salvage the* Wallaces. *Such tugs were vital cogs in the machinery of normal port operations including wrecking when the need arose. Author*

steering from astern, she was brought into the harbor stern first and allowed to settle to the bottom next to the old Burtis Dock in the same place the *Wallaces* moored the year before. Bringing her in stern first was likely the result of rudder damage as well as trying to keep undue pressure off a large hole in her bow otherwise a single tug could have done the job. Since the hole was "repaired" by a diver stuffing several old horse blankets into it, the need to keep the pressure off is apparent.

Steam pumps were soon hoisted aboard the *Bradley* and her cargo removed. On Monday, November 13, the *S.E. Sheldon* took the *Bradley* in tow and headed for the Soo but it was a troublesome trip. The next day off Au Sable Point the steamer was making her way through a moderate northwest gale when the massive bolts securing the engine journal broke! Luckily the steamer *W.H. Stephens* saw the wildly drifting vessels and took both in tow and safely reached the Soo. Doubtless she also received a salvage award for her timely intervention!

The *Bradley* continued in service until October 13, 1884 when she sprang a leak in a gale and sank seven miles southwest of North Manitou Island in northern Lake Michigan.

She had been ashore near Grand Island off Munising, Lake Superior three years prior to her Marquette sojourn but hauled free without major damage. Shot Point, however, was her end. Bits and pieces of her hull can still be found in the shallows offshore as well as on the beach after north gales.

References:

Annual Report US Life-Saving Service - 1888 pp. 145-146.

Daily Mining Journal, May 30, July 5, 1885, October 24, 29, November 3, 5, 8, 12, 19, December 3, 10, 1887, March 17, 31, May 12, June 9, 23, September 22, 1888.

Duluth Tribune, October 14, 1882.

John Mansfield, *History of the Great Lakes*. J.H. Beers and Company, Chicago, 1899.

Marine Directory of the Great Lakes. R. Polk and Company, 1884.

Merchant Vessels of the United States, 1886, 1894.

Runge Collection, Milwaukee Public Library - *Plymouth*.

Lake Carriers Annual - 1913.

Into the Breakers - the *Charles J. Kershaw*

After the second set of wrecks the need for a station at Marquette was unquestioned by Kimball and in 1891 it was finally fully operational. *(See Inset for details, page 111 - Station Marquette.)*

Keeper Henry J. Cleary, previously keeper at the Deer Park Life-Saving Station on the Shipwreck Coast, was selected to take command of the new facility. *(More details on inset page 113 - Cleary.)*

Cleary and his crew proved their worth in September 1895. On the morning of the 28th the 223-foot wooden steamer *Charles J. Kershaw* was upbound for the city towing the schooner-barges *Henry A. Kent* and *Moonlight*. Schooner-barges were old sailing schooners with their top hamper cut down and crews reduced to the bare minimum needed to operate.

Dark clouds filled the horizon and occasional bolts of lightning reflected eerily off the lake and back to the base of the low clouds. Captain Pringle on the bridge of the *Kershaw*, knew a good storm was bearing down on them but there wasn't too far to go before reaching the safety of the harbor at Marquette.

The steamer Charles J. Kershaw *entering the port of Conneaut, Ohio, on Lake Erie in 1892. Author*

By noon the storm was still in the distance, as if baiting them to continue farther into the lake before snapping shut. Oddly, the wind blew south instead of hauling sharply north as Pringle expected. Still the seas were sloppy but nothing dangerous and he was making good time so he kept on for Marquette. At 10:00 p.m. the south wind veered quickly northeast and soon reached gale force. Pringle rang chief engineer McEachren deep in the bowels of the ship asking for more revolutions from her 400 horsepower steam engine. The nor'east wind was blowing them toward shore and he needed the power to claw out into deeper water.

Powerful seas slammed hard into the quarter of *Kershaw*, sending gray combers of cold water streaming down the length of her deck. She rolled and pitched like a wild thing, responding as best she could the tumultuous seas. The schooner-barges were having an equally rough time, reacting to the pounding like puppets on a string, one minute cresting high on a wave and the next surfing down the front.

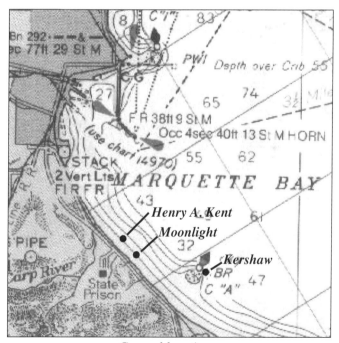

General locations.

Torrents of driving rain blinded the ships from seeing anything useful. The steamer could only continue on by compass and log and the schooner-barges trusting their fate to the steamer.

Down in the engineroom trouble was brewing. Chief McEachren braced himself up against a stanchion and calmly watched a chain wrapped steam pipe a couple of feet in front of him. Up on deck it was freezing cold but in the engineroom the roaring boiler and hissing steam made it into a veritable sauna bath. Sweat rolled off his brow and dripped from his nose. Still the stoker continued to shovel coal into the boiler. Coal meant fire, which meant heat, which meant more steam, which meant more power for the wheezing steam engine and that's what the old man called for. Concealed beneath the cinched tight chain was a very thin crack perhaps a foot long. Already steam was hissing out along its jagged length. Luckily the engineer saw the crack in enough time to chain'er up but how long she would hold was anyone's guess, especially with the captain's demand for more power.

The pipe held out for a long time, almost long enough for the steamer to reach Marquette. They only needed another ten minutes or so and all would be safe but at 2:40 p.m. just as she was rounding the breakwater into the lower harbor and in the flash of the light, it let go

The Henry A. Kent *on the beach shortly after the storm. Author*

with an explosion of chain and iron pipe fragments. Without the churning propeller the *Kershaw* and her two charges were at the mercy of the gale and the gale had no mercy!

Pringle immediately ordered distress signals burned and cutting the towing hawser to the schooner-barges. They would fare better separately than bound together. All three ships were soon being driven by wind and wave to the nearby beach. Within minutes the steamer lost sight of the schooner-barges in the stygian darkness.

With the deathly scrape of wood on rock the *Kershaw* struck at 3:00 a.m. on a reef about 3/4 mile off the Chocolay River, right at the eastern edge of the city limits. Immediately, huge waves began to roll over the dying steamer. Her bow showed a gaping black hole where she first smashed into the reef and water flooded in. Pringle and his crew huddled forlornly in the stern, unable to raise a hand to save their own lives.

The watchman in the Marquette Life-Saving Service Station lookout tower first spotted the Kershaw's *distress signals. Nelson Collection*

The *Moonlight* and *Kent* were far luckier than the *Kershaw*. Both drifted before the gale until fetching up broadside on the beach just inward of the *Kershaw* reef. They were driven so far ashore their crews could leap to the beach without getting their feet wet!

The *Kershaw* was lucky, too, but in a different way. While she was battling around the breakwater one of Cleary's surfman was on watch in the lookout tower. Regardless of how miserable the weather was, the tower was always manned by a sharp-eyed surfman. When

Pringle had distress signals burned, the surfman saw them and alerted his crewmates. Within five minutes Life-Savers were tumbling out of warm dry bunks and assembling their gear. Fifteen minutes later an eight horse team was hitched to the wagon carrying their surfboat and they were marching for the beach Cleary knew the steamer would hit. It was a miserable trek of several miles through swamp, brush and sand and all the while they were lashed by the storm. By the time the first glimmer of dawn began to turn black into dark gray, the Life-Savers determined the *Moonlight* and *Kent* were safe but the men on the steamer needed help and fast! Cleary assembled his men on the beach opposite the *Kershaw* and prepared to launch their surfboat. What the surfmen saw was nothing short of horrifying.

This photo illustrates the difference between the big lifeboat on the left and smaller surfboat on the right. The lifeboat was designed to smash through the waves and was virtually unsinkable. By contrast the surfboat was fast and nimble, intended for lighter work. Cleary of Marquette is at the rudder of the lifeboat and the crew likely those men who rescued the Kershaw *crew. Author*

Into the breakers, a Life-Saving Service crew heads out for a rescue!
Author

Between the impaled steamer and shore the lake was a maelstrom of tossing debris. Old driftwood and stumps pulled from the beach by the grasping seas, logs lost from raft booms and pieces of the *Kershaw* itself all boiled together in wicked splendor. It was a hell-spawned sea of death and a terrible gauntlet the Life-Savers would have to brave to reach the steamer.

To put the sea conditions into proper perspective the official station journal for the 29th marked the surf "very high." Regulations required the Life-Savers to mark sea conditions every six hours using ten increasing levels of danger. "Very high" was the tenth, or worst intensity.

The Life-Savers made their first launch at 7:00 a.m. By this time word of the wreck spread throughout the city and hundreds of people gathered on the shore to watch the surfmen in action. Cleary and his crew didn't disappoint them. As soon as the surfboat launched into the lake she and the surfmen were instantly inundated with sheets of freezing water. Waves literally swallowed the frail craft but each time she rose like a cork and continued gamely on for the wreck. Time and again the sharp bow knifed into living waves of rolling white water and with oars biting deeply into nothing but air, was driven backward toward the beach. Recovering, the little boat continued on for the *Kershaw*.

Once they reached the dying steamer, Cleary carefully brought the surfboat under the protection of the lee in the stern. Nine sailors quickly slid down a rope into the wildly bobbing surfboat. Captain Pringle and three men were left aboard for a second trip.

Pulling hard for the beach, the surfboat filled several times with water when crashing seas swept over her stern. Each time, the self-bailing surfboat spewed water from her freeing ports and crawled on beetle-like for shore. Cleary carefully guided her close to the beach but a mass of flotsam required several surfmen to jump into the freezing water to clear a path for her. As a result, surfman Joe Greenwood was crushed in the jam of logs before she landed. But the sailors from the *Kershaw* were safe ashore. The sailors and injured surfman were quickly taken to Marquette's St. Mary's Hospital.

When Cleary prepared to launch again the injured surfman's place was taken by a local volunteer. Using volunteers wasn't all that unusual. In many instances they were former surfmen but always very competent boatmen. Once more the surfboat shot out into the wild lake. Huge logs and splintered wreckage surged to and fro in the waves as she slowly crawled again toward the steamer. Within thirty yards of the wreck she was struck by three vicious waves in quick succession. The first two were safely ridden out. The third broached her and she capsized. Unfazed, the Life-Savers righted her only to be hammered by another wave again shoving her keel skyward. Again they righted her and again she rolled. Caught in the trough of the waves it was a vicious cycle. Only years of hard drilling under Cleary's sharp eyes gave the men the professionalism needed to keep fighting back, keep struggling to make the rescue. Death may not have ridden the boat that day, but it was never far away.

Finally a large piece of wreckage smashed hard into the surfboat damaging it too much to continue and knocking surfmen Patrick Connors and Harry Gibbs unconscious. Other crewman grabbed onto the pair and all rode the boat ashore. Both men were bundled off to the hospital.

The surfmen knew the rules. They knew they couldn't quit. The motto was a constant reminder..." Regulations say we have to go out… they say nothing about coming back." Cleary and the uninjured members of the crew returned to the station for the big 34-foot lifeboat. The two boats were as different as different could be. The small 24-foot surfboat weighted perhaps 900 pounds. Nimble and very seaworthy it was the preferred method of making a near shore rescue. By contrast the lifeboat tipped the scales at perhaps 4,000 pounds but was considered virtually unsinkable. Where the surfboat dashed through the waves, the lifeboat battered through them. She was perfect for deepwater work far at sea. Both had their place in the Life-Saver's arsenal.

It was about this time the steamer began to break in two. The sailors left aboard lowered their small yawl and leaped it, holding it alongside the lee of the steamer. Even so protected it kept swamping and the men were forced to keep bailing to stay afloat. Using it to reach the beach was not even a consideration, especially when they knew the Life-Savers would be back. They never quit on a rescue.

Back at the Life-Saving station Cleary and his men, augmented with volunteers to replace the newly injured surfmen, ran the big lifeboat down the boathouse ramp and into the harbor. They would have to row the three and a half miles to get to the wreck.

The ad hoc lifeboat crew strained at the oars for all they were worth with Cleary constantly admonishing them to "put their backs into it!" The big lifeboat tossed from wave crest to wave crest, all the time moving inexorably toward the *Kershaw*. The men in the lifeboat pulled at the long 14-foot oars until their backs screamed with agony, especially the volunteers who were unused to the terrific effort. Reaching the wreck, Cleary deftly brought the lifeboat into the lee and plucked the half-drowned sailors from their nearly swamped yawl. For an agonizing moment Cleary considered rowing back to the station but a long look at his nearly all-in volunteers convinced him his only choice was to make a beach landing next to the damaged surfboat. Running the lifeboat through the breakers and morass of wreckage was dangerous but his skill was equal to the job and the big lifeboat slid safely up on the beach.

The local newspaper, the *Marquette Mining Journal* proclaimed the rescue, " …as plucky and skillful a piece of work on the part of all

Captain Henry Cleary and the Marquette Life-Saving Service Station crew. The station still stands today. Marquette Maritime Museum

concerned as the shores of Lake Superior have ever seen, or as the gallant annals of the Life-Saving Service can boast."

Today we can read the words describing the rescue but can't comprehend what they really mean. Our daily frame of reference no longer includes maneuvering a surfboat in wild surf or a lifeboat battering through crashing waves. While we can intellectually understand the action without the experience of seeing it, we can't truly appreciate it. This is our loss as it defines courage, skill and the triumph of the human spirit.

On returning to the station the Life-Savers were so exhausted and depleted by the injured men, Cleary didn't send out the north beach patrol, normally conducted from the station north along the shore for four miles.

Pringle would experience shipwreck just over a year later. On October 1896 he was captain of the 282-foot wooden steamer *Australasia* in Lake Michigan when she caught fire off Baileys Harbor on the Wisconsin side of the lake. Since she was loaded with soft coal there was some apparent urgency in extinguishing the blaze. However, the crew seems to have immediately lowered the lifeboat and rowed to shore landing in the village of Jacksonport. The ship was left to her fate. The men ran off so quickly they literally left their dinner on the table. Two hours later a tugboat appeared on the scene and put a salvage crew aboard the deserted steamer. The tug men found the uneaten meal, said "what the hell," sat down and had a quick bite before checking the still burning fire. After enjoying an unexpected repast, they passed a hawser to the tug and hauled her into port, eventually grounding her in shallow water. The tug figured the steamers crew ended up in Jacksonport since it was the closest place with a bar so she landed to pick them up. However, the steamer's men had enough time to really get their "steam up" and a brawl broke out on the tug during the run to Sturgeon Bay. Perhaps one of the tug men questioned the courage of the steamboat men. For Pringle though, it was two shipwrecks in two years and each a total loss![4]

The *Kershaw* wreck and rescue was a great tourist attraction with folks coming from far and wide for a good look. Local liverymen weren't able to supply enough carriages to meet demand and by 2:00 p.m. not a single horse was left in any local stable.

The *Kershaw* was built in 1874 in Bangor, Michigan and enrolled in Port Huron in May of that year. Owned by an Ohio syndicate with William S. Mack of Cleveland as the principal stockholder, she was 1,324 gross tons, 233-feet overall, 37-feet in beam and 16-feet in depth. As common during the period she also had three masts. If the weather was fair, canvas could help propel her. She was valued at $40,000.

The 206-foot *Moonlight* was built in Milwaukee the same year by Wolff and Davidson. Also Mack owned, she was mastered by a Captain Peterson and valued at $23,000. The 195-foot *Henry A. Kent*, owned by Warner of Cleveland and mastered by Captain Hunt, was built in 1873 at Detroit and valued at $16,000.

Of the three ships, the *Moonlight* was by far the most famous. When she came out of the builder's ways she was one of the most remarkable vessels on the Great Lakes. She was the biggest ever attempted by Wolf and Davidson with a capacity of 50,000 bushels of grain, 6,000 more than any previous vessel built at Milwaukee. And she was fast! Her vast sail rig allowed her to carry a huge spread of canvas for a three-master. Unusual for a lake schooner she also carried

The Moonlight *was one of the most famous schooners on the lakes before being reduced to a schooner-barge. Author*

a figurehead, in her case a half-moon under her bowsprit. Over 500 people watched her launching. She immediately entered the lucrative Milwaukee to Buffalo grain trade.

Her first captain was Denis Sullivan, an Irishman who arrived in Milwaukee via Canada. A mere 25 years old when he assumed command he had a reputation as a driver, a man capable of wringing every knot out of a ship he could. And he did, the *Moonlight* leaving many lesser vessels bobbing along in her wake. In the 1876 season she set a record of 21 round trips between Milwaukee and Buffalo with grain.

By 1899 she was out of the lucrative grain trade and sold to a group of Cleveland Merchants led by William S. Mack for use in the workaday business of hauling iron ore down from Lake Superior. Her lofty sail rig was cut down relegating her to the role of schooner-barge.

William Mack immediately surrendered the *Kershaw, Moonlight* and *Kent* to the underwriters for the insured value of $39,000. He wanted no part of trying to salvage them. It was better to take the insurance money and move on.

The *Kershaw* was a total loss wedged between the two sections of the reef. The bow was gone, broken off by the waves shortly after the Life-Savers saved the crew. During the following days the relentless waves smashed the steamer into pieces. But the schooner-barges could be dragged off the beach and sail again. The initial contract for salvage was awarded to the Grummond Towing and Wrecking Company of Detroit. The company immediately sent their big wrecking tug *Swain* to Marquette and soon she was using her propeller to blow a channel through the sand shallows to reach the wrecks. It was a good plan but didn't work. As the tug slowly backed to the wrecks, "eating" her way through the sand, the swirling grains simply washed around in front of the ship in the area already dredge and settled to the bottom. Soon the tug was trapped in her own channel! The tug *Gillett* from Marquette came out and using the same technique as the *Swain* but with better results, blew a channel open freeing her.

By November 1 the Grummond Company gave up the salvage contract to the B.B. Inman Company of Duluth. Inman responded to the challenge by sending the company tugs *Pearl B. Campbell*, *Edward Fisk*, *M.B. Carrington* and *Record* to Marquette. Captain Inman was certain the *Kent* would be free in a day if he had good weather.

Good weather on Superior in the late fall is always an iffy thing and plagued by wind and wave the wreckers made scant progress. The *Mining Journal* complained both vessels would soon go to pieces if the wreckers didn't hurry and get them off the beach. When the weather finally provided an opportunity, Inman put all five tugs and a dredge to work digging a channel to the *Kent* alone. He couldn't cut a channel any closer to the wreck than 30 feet! Inman was moved to comment in disgust, "It is an utter impossibility to get the schooners off. They are doomed to go to pieces on the beach where they stand." He packed up his tugs and went back to Duluth.

Perhaps it was all just a negotiating ploy by Inman since he was back in the city by November 23 with a new contract, a considerable improvement over the old one. Now he would receive $9,500 if he had both vessels in Duluth by February 1. If he only had the *Kent*, his fee was reduced to $5,000. Trying got him nothing. This was a "no cure, no pay" contract. For two weeks he attempted to haul them off the beach. No sooner did he dredge a channel right up to them than a storm rolled in and filled it in again with sand. Finally he succeeded in getting a 16-foot channel right up to the *Kent* only to discover her keel

The Moonlight *(left) and* Henry A. Kent *(right) during salvage operations. Note the smoke belching dredge on the extreme right. Author*

was fast in gravel. Since his pumps couldn't handle gravel, he again quit the job. It was two weeks of work without a nickel of return.

On December 21 the underwriters sold the twin wrecks to Captain Jay Hursley of the Hursley Tug Line from Sault Ste. Marie for $7,000. It seems Hursley, after carefully examining the wrecks, asked the underwriters for an immediate contract to free them but they replied the earliest they would issue a contract was the spring, if at all. Given the severity of the winter there was no guarantee anything would be left of either vessel. Convinced he could quickly free them, Hursley took a gamble and bought them immediately for $7,000.

A week later Hursley arrived in Marquette by train with two special steam pumps. Chartering the tugs *Gillette* and *City Of Marquette* he went right to work experimenting with different approaches to the problem. Apparently satisfied with the results, he left a caretaker on the *Moonlight* and returned to the Soo for the winter.

Early in May he was back in Marquette with the small steamer *City Of Grand Rapids* and tugs *Corona* and *Edward Fisk* and went directly to work on the vessels still intact after a mild winter. On May 10, he had the *Moonlight* off the beach and eleven days later the *Kent* also. After some quick caulking of split seams he send both to Cleveland for refitting under tow of the tug *Gillen*.

Hursley achieved a great return on his investment. Adding $4,500 in salvage costs to the $7,000 purchase price meant an outlay of $11,500. The *Moonlight* alone later sold for $25,000 to Captain Joseph Gilchrist of Cleveland for his fleet. The captain from the Soo turned a fine profit doing what one wrecker said was "utterly impossible."

Gilchrist ran the *Moonlight,* hauling Lake Superior ore for a few years then in 1899 took advantage of the tremendous boom in the Atlantic coast coal trade to charter the *Moonlight* and *David Wallace* to the Atlantic Transportation Company of New York for saltwater service. The pair reached the east coast via the Welland Canal around Niagara Falls and the St. Lawrence River. By August, 1900, she was back in Cleveland, her saltwater sojourn completed.

The *Kent's* career was a short one after her Marquette adventure. On September 17, 1897, she was downbound from Ashland with iron ore and taking on water in a gale off Stannard's Rock. The situation was serious enough that around midnight the towing steamer *G. C.*

Gilchrist dropped the towing hawser and circled back to pick up her crew and passengers. It took Captain William Battner three tries to lay up to the sinking *Kent* long enough to allow those aboard to climb over to the steamer but he finally pulled the very difficult feat off. Not long after, everyone was safe on the steamer including the captain's three children, the *Kent* dove for the bottom.

The *Moonlight* lasted until September 13, 1903 when she foundered in a terrific gale off Michigan Island in the Apostles group. Her tow steamer, the *Volunteer* took off her crew before she dove for the bottom. Her loss was considered the passing of an era. An old time captain said, " The *Moonlight*, at the time she was built, was considered one of the finest sailing vessels on the lakes. She was a pretty vessel and was very fast, being able to sail rings around the other boats. When under full sail she was a beauty."

It is fascinating to note the *Moonlight* was the seventh Gilchrist vessel wrecked in 1903. This is especially interesting as Gilchrist was usually self-insured; he carried all the risk himself without the protection of underwriting companies. The advantage was he didn't pay anyone any premiums. The disadvantage, of course, was should there be an accident he didn't have the security of insurance. Quite by chance in 1903 he purchased policies on the older vessels in his fleet and then either disaster or fortune struck, depending on one's point of view. Consider the following litany of loss: June, the *John Craig* was heavily damaged after stranding on Simmons Reef in Lake Michigan; July, the wood propeller *V. Swain* sank at her dock in Superior on Lake Superior; July 22, the wooden steamer *Waverly* sank off Harbor Beach in Lake Huron; September 15, the steamer *A.A. Parker* sank off Grand Marais, Lake Superior; October 15, the wooden steamer *Marquette* sank off the Apostle Islands, Lake Superior and on October 26, the wooden steamer *Manhattan* wrecked on a reef at Grand Island, Lake Superior. Gilchrist certainly knew when to carry insurance!

Captain Robert Pringle of the *Kershaw* later went on to found the Pringle Barge Line of Sandusky, Ohio. A major asset of the line was the 101-foot steam tug *Robert C. Pringle*, previously the *Chequamegon*, renamed from the *Pere Marquette* built 1903 in Manitowoc, Wisconsin. He was aboard her when she waterlogged and sank in 1922 after striking an unknown obstruction 15 miles off

Manitowoc. She was towing the propeller *Venezuela* from Milwaukee to Sandusky for repairs. There were no casualties.

While the two schooner-barges are long gone from the Marquette scene, the remains of the *Kershaw* are still laying around on the bottom of the lake as well as in various garages and basements. Since the advent of sport diving she has been a popular attraction, her bits and pieces spread out over several acres of bottom in depths ranging from 25-35 feet. The broken condition of the hull can be partially explained by a 1902 salvager from the Soo who used dynamite to blast the wreck apart to scrounge her ironwork.

References:

Annual Report, U.S. Life-Saving Service - 1896, pp. 88-89.

Brendon Baillod, "Historical Section for Inclusion on the National Register of Historic Places Schooner *Moonlight*," Unpublished manuscript, Baillod Collection.

R.A. Brotherton, "The Wreck of the *Kershaw, Moonlight* and *Kent*" *Inland Seas*, Summer 1848, pp. 124-126.

Certificate of Enrollment, U.S. Customs Department, May 14, 1874.

Paul J. Creviere, Jr. *Wild Gales and Tattered Sails* (Paul J. Creviere, Jr, 1997), pp. 162-164.

Daily Mining Journal, October 5, 12, November 2,9, 23, 30, December 7, 14, 21, 23, 28, 1895, May 23, 39, 1896.

Journal of the Lighthouse at Marquette, May 10, 1896.

Journal of the Marquette Life-Saving Station, September 29 - 30, 1895.

Sault Evening News, September 15, 1903.

Kershaw File - Stonehouse Collection.

Footnotes:

[1] This is a good number for 1915 when the Life-Saving Service combined with the U.S. Revenue Marine to form the new Coast Guard. During the 44 year history of the Service total stations were somewhat higher at various times.

[2] Hogged is a term applied to a ship when its bow and stern have drooped.

[3] There is some confusion over the use of the barrels. The *Marquette Mining Journal* is the source for the information I used. Dave Swayze in his outstanding Shipwreck Data section of www.boatnerd.com states the *Plymouth* was moved from the rocks by combining jacks, a very common salvage method with a frame with 200 air-filled kerosene barrels secured to the wreck. The common factor is using air filled barrels.

[4] Another version claims the steamer sand east of Cana Island and her crew was removed by Life-Savers.

Marquette - The Life-Saving Station

The most important federal contribution to Marquette area maritime safety was the establishment of a U.S. Life-Saving Service Station in the city. Although the Marquette station wasn't opened until 1891, the first substantial steps toward establishing the station were made two years before.

In July 1889 two representatives of the Life-Saving Service visited Marquette to determine the actual station location. After surveying the coast between the Chocolay River and Presque Isle, the pair decided the federal lighthouse reservation land at Lighthouse Point was the best. However for that site to be fully suitable, the station boathouse and launchway had to be constructed on land just inside the breakwater, near the City Waterworks dock. The dock was used to unload coal for the waterworks steam pumps.

Although the Life-Saving Service and Lighthouse Service were both agencies of the Treasury Department, they were not linked in any formal fashion. While the overall mission of both involved maritime safety, the lighthouse keepers only had to assure their lamp was burning and fog signal blowing if needed to accomplish their mission. No personal risk was required. By contrast, the Life-Savers were expected to perform rescues in the most hazardous of circumstance, often at great risk to their lives. In rare instances the two were collocated as at Marquette. More commonly they were widely distant.

It was critical that the launchway for the station's boats be located in an area that would allow the crew to launch regardless of the weather. With the exception of the Waterworks land, the rest of the shoreline was open and exposed to wave action. By contrast the Waterworks site, sheltered by the breakwater, offered a launch without trouble and full headway could be gained by the boat crew before the lifeboat reached the open lake.

Since the City owned the property application was made to the City Water Board for permission to use the land. The Board, including venerable Peter White, quickly agreed, clearing the way for station construction.

The Life-Saving Service Station was authorized by the previous Congress after a strong local lobbying effort. There was ample reason for Marquette's eagerness for a station since the area had been the site of numerous shipwrecks. Of particular note were the triple wrecks of 1886 and 1887.

The boat drills Cleary and his crew conducted were of special interest. Large crowds often watched as they brought a boat out into the harbor exercising the men in capsizing and quickly righting it. During an actual rescue the ability to bring her back up in the midst of boiling seas could mean life or death for shipwreck victims as well as surfmen. The capsizing drill was especially popular during the July 4th festival.

Marquette Station was considered one of the best in the Life-Saving Service and due to their high regard, Cleary and his crew were selected for a special assignment. In September 1899 they collaborated with the Lake Shore Engine Works of Marquette to develop and test the first motorized lifeboat in the Service. The engine, a two cylinder 12 horsepower model, was able to propel the lifeboat very effectively. Most of the actual modification work to the lifeboat was accomplished by Cleary and his Number One surfman, John Anderson. Both had extensive boat building experience and constructed small craft in their off time. Eventually all Service boats were motorized based on the Marquette model.

The Keeper - Henry Cleary

Throughout its days as a Life-Saving Station, 1891 - 1915, Marquette had only one keeper, Henry J. Cleary. A native of Port Hope, Michigan on the shores of Lake Huron, he sailed on a schooner for several years before joining the Life-Saving Service at Point aux Barques at age 19. He later served at nearby Grindstone City and Tawas before being transferred to lonely Deer Park on Lake Superior's "Shipwreck Coast" as keeper in 1885. He remained at Deer Park until transferring to Marquette to open the new station.

Cleary was very highly regarded by the Service and he was selected above all other keepers to train the demonstration Life-Saving Service crew for the 1893 Chicago Worlds Fair. As a way of generating good publicity, the Service regularly erected model Life-Saving Stations and provided demonstration crews to all of the great national expositions. Cleary trained the crews, which were made up of selected

Henry Cleary and his crew circa 1910. They were the "Storm Warriors" of Marquette. Author

Cleary and his demonstration crew at the 1898 Trans-Mississippi Exposition and Indian Congress in Omaha, Nebraska. The crew was composed of surfmen selected from stations throughout the Service. The Apache war chief Geronimo is standing at the stern next to Cleary. Geronimo apparently got along well with Cleary and his men. Institute for Great Lakes Research

men from stations throughout the service, for the Trans-Mississippi Exposition in Omaha 1898, Pan-American Exposition in Buffalo 1901, Louisiana Purchase Exposition in St. Louis 1904, Jamestown Exposition in Hampton Roads 1907, and Alaska-Yukon-Pacific Exposition in Seattle 1909. Cleary's crews demonstrated their expertise before millions of spectators and he had the opportunity to meet world civilian and military leaders.

Cleary was far more than just show, although his work at the national expositions earned him the title of "Showman of the Service." He was a superb boat handler and a Life-Saver keeper without peer as he demonstrated with the rescue of the crew of the steamer *Pacific* at Deer Park and *Kershaw* in Marquette.

An innovator, too, he was vital to the development of motorized boats for the Service.

Cleary died of pneumonia at the station on April 10, 1916. He was 54 years old and a 37-year veteran of the Service, 25 of them at Marquette.

A Life-Saving Legend – Albert Ocha

If anyone was born to be a Life-Saver it was Albert Ocha. He sprang into the world on April 5, 1863 and soon after his parents settled in Port Hope, Michigan on Lake Huron. Port Hope was Henry Cleary's home town, too, but whether the families knew each other is speculative. When Albert was old enough he started work as a boat builder but decided it wasn't the career for him although he learned a great deal about small craft, knowledge that he later found vital.

On March 21, 1882 the strapping 18 year old signed on with the Life-Saving Service. The job promised travel, at least away from Port Hope and adventure. He was a big husky youth, well muscled with broad shoulders and a square face. And he could certainly pull an oar. He was first assigned to the station at Ottawa Point, later renamed

Tawas Point, Lake Huron. Ocha learned his job fast and must have impressed the district superintendent since on October 9, 1886 he was appointed keeper at the new station at Portage Entry on Lake Superior. He was a mere 23 years old!

He met his first wife, a widow with three children, while stationed at Portage Entry. Apparently, she bore him a daughter but the marriage was a short one. Whether it ended in divorce or her death is unclear. About 1890 he met and married a local gal from the nearby mining town of Lake Linden, Georgiana Fountaine. A son was born soon after.

Albert Ocha was one of the great legendary keepers of the old Life-Saving Service. Hemp Collection

The why is unknown but in July, 1892 he was transferred to Grande Point Au Sable station on Lake Michigan. In December, 1893 he resigned from the Service. Why he left is also unknown but in 1893 the country was in the midst of a major depression and the very low pay of the Service was causing many good men to leave. That year alone an estimated 30 per cent of the Life-Savers on the Great Lakes resigned to find better paying jobs that could provide for their families!

Ocha must have missed the Service dearly because the following year he signed on as a surfman at the Ashabula, Ohio station on Lake Erie. In 1896 he was up at Crisp's Point on Lake Superior, again as surfman. He stayed there until the station closed for the winter in 1899.It is possible to speculate there may have been some "institutional bias" against a former keeper returning to the Service after quitting. During this period two more sons and a daughter were born. Maintaining a family in such a difficult location as Crisp's, one of the four remote Shipwreck Coast stations, was extremely difficult. Medical care was nonexistent as was any social life beyond the company of the small Life-Saving community. The nearest town of any size was Grand Marais, nearly 35 miles westward. And when the snows of winter lay deep across the Northwoods, communication of any kind virtually ceased.

In 1900 Ocha was appointed keeper of another of the desolate Shipwreck Coast stations, at the Two-Heart River to the west of Crisp's Point. Financially, it was a significant boost in pay from the $40 a month of surfman (season only) to $900 a year. But it was still a very small salary for the responsibility and sacrifice necessary. His wife bore him four more children at Two-Heart and one, a girl, died in infancy and was buried in the little station cemetery. In February, 1910 his wife was pregnant again and as her time neared she needed immediate medical care. In the middle of a blizzard Ocha trekked to Grand Marais, the closest town with a doctor and nearly 25 miles away! The Grand Marais doctor wouldn't dare battle the blizzard to go to the isolated station, waiting instead for the storm to blow itself out. By the time Ocha and doctor reached Georgiana, she was dead. Ocha was now a single parent. He kept his brood together but as they grew his children, as expected, went their own way. His oldest son joined the Life-Saving crew at Grand Marais and another shipped out on a lake freighter. His oldest daughter worked as his housekeeper and cook. The others all helped where they could.

In early 1912 Ocha was appointed keeper of the new Life-Saving Station at Eagle Harbor on the Keweenaw Peninsula. It was the last station ever built on the Great Lakes. He died at the station on November 22, 1912. In the parlance of mariners of the time, "he crossed the bar." It is believed liver failure was the cause but at only 49 years old, it is reasonable to say he just wore himself out in the Service. Two days later he was buried at the Pinegrove Cemetery in Eagle Harbor on the opposite side of the harbor from the station. His body was conveyed to it's final resting place by the motor surfboat as a waterborne hearse, his crew serving as pallbearers. A temporary surfman, hired to fill Ocha's place on the roster, remained in the tower keeping a silent watch on the lakeshore.

References:

Annual Report of the US Life-Saving Service - 1886-1912.

Daily Mining Gazette, November 23, 1912.

Albert Ocha File - Stonehouse Collection.

County of Keweenaw, Pinegrove Cemetery -
www.mfhn.com/keweenaw/achivestemp/pinegrove_3.txt.

* **7**

ELMA

Climb The Rocks

Early fall gales, harbingers of storms yet to come, lashed the Great Lakes during the last days of September, 1895. Vessels took shelter wherever they could. The steamer *Westover* with the schooner-barge *A.T. Bliss* in tow barely made safe harbor in Manitowoc on Lake Michigan. Both were heavily damaged from the storm, the *Bliss* losing her deck load of lumber as well as main and foremasts. At St. Joseph the steamer *Puritian*, running from Chicago, got within three miles of the harbor but had to turn back. The seas were running so high over the breakwaters she refused to chance an entrance. On Lake Huron the Reid tugs *Mockingbird* and *Reliance* battled with their huge log raft finally bringing it to safe haven under Lookout Point near Tawas City. In Lake Ontario two schooners rolled helpless under the breakwater at Buffalo. Across the lake at Port Colborne, Ontario the schooner *Paul* struggled in to shelter with her bulwarks, jib, mainmast and foresail carried away by the icy blasts. Another schooner had her hooks down six miles out from the breakwater while distress flags stood iron hard at her mizzen. It was far too dangerous for anyone from shore to even think of a rescue.

To many observers the worst of the damage was on Lake Superior. The steamer *Charles J. Kershaw* and her consorts *Moonlight* and *Kent* were making their way to Marquette in spite of the rolling gale bashing them unmercifully. The city and safety was just a couple of miles distant when a critical steam pipe burst in the *Kershaw* sending her and her consorts to the tender mercy of wind and wave. But wind and wave don't have mercy! The consorts ended up on the beach but the *Kershaw* drove hard on a rock reef several hundred yards off shore.

It took a tremendous effort by the crew of the Marquette Life-Saving Service Station to save the crew of the steamer. Luckily the men were available to do the difficult job. Other ships in desperate trouble other places didn't have the "storm warriors" of the Life-Saving Service to come to their aid.

Conditions at the Pictured Rocks 30 miles east of Marquette were just as bad. The steamer *Walluda*, towing a whaleback barge, was battered by the gale so heavily she took shelter behind Grand Island. The *Walluda* had five feet of water sloshing around in her holds and her clanking steam pumps could just keep up with the flood. Had she stayed out on the lake, sinking would have been the likely result.

The schooner-barge *Elma*, together with the schooner-barges *Chester B. Jones* and *Commodore*, had departed Pequaming, Michigan under tow of the steamer *P. H. Birckhead* on Wednesday, September 25.

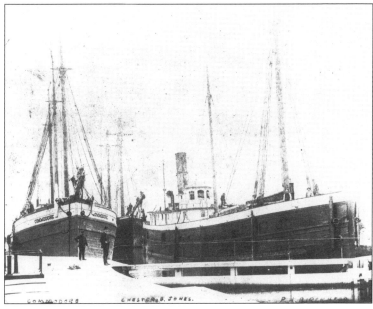

The schooner-barges Commodore *and* Chester B. Jones *and steamer* P.H. Birckhead. *Rutherford B. Hayes Presidential Library*

Pequaming was a small lumber town about 40 miles west of Marquette. All four ships carried large loads of newly milled lumber consigned to markets in the lower lakes. The *Birckhead* was considered a powerful steamer with a reputation for pulling large tows. On Thursday the *Birckhead* and her string took shelter in Marquette from the rough weather. When the lake calmed down on Friday evening, the *Birckhead* took her charges in tow and left to continue down the lakes.

The calm however was short lived. By the time the group was off Whitefish Point on Saturday, about 120 miles west of Marquette, the lake was roiled by full lake nor'wester. The *Birckhead* intended to bring her consorts to anchor under the shelter of the east side of Whitefish Point but the stress of the storm snapped the towline from the steamer to the first schooner-barge. The loose string was now controlled by the powerful blasts of the storm. One by one they dropped the hawser connecting them together to face the storm alone. There was no other choice.

The loss of the towing hawser is not a reason to panic. Such things happened before so the crews on the schooner-barges stood by waiting to see if the steamer would try to pass another to them. But in the prevailing gale getting a hawser to all of them would be well neigh impossible.

The *Jones* was in the most danger, being blown to within a mile and a half of the beach west of Whitefish Point before her anchors caught, keeping her just out of the deadly breakers of the outer bar.

The Life-Savers first learned of the schooner-barge's deadly predicament early in the morning of the 29th when John Clarke of Whitefish Point telephoned Captain Samuel Bernier of the Vermilion Station with the news. Clarke recommended Bernier bring his beach apparatus. John operated cranberry farms near Vermilion at nearby Little Lake. Vermilion Point is about eight miles west of Whitefish Point and the nearest station to the imperiled vessel. A series of four Life-Saving Service stations were built west of Whitefish Point in 1877; going east to west, Vermilion Point, Crisp's Point, Two-Heart River and Deer Park. No Life-Saving Station was ever at Whitefish Point.

The beach apparatus consisted of a two-wheeled cart containing the gear, including a small bronze gun called a Lyle gun after it's inventor, needed to rig a breaches buoy from shore to the wreck. The cart

The Vermilion Point Life-Saving Station was a small oasis of civilization on a wild and forbidding shore. Author

weighed roughly 900 pounds fully loaded and was normally hauled by hand. Since the wreck was roughly six miles to the east, Bernier telephoned Crisp's Point Life-Saving Station, the next station to the west, approximately eight miles distant and asked for the team of horses kept there. The team arrived at Vermilion at 1:30 p.m. Within fifteen minutes Bernier and his six-man crew had the apparatus hitched up and were underway over the storm swept beaches to Whitefish Point. It was a miserable trip. Not only were they fighting the wind and rain with occasional hail but also deep sand and in places forced to wade storm swollen streams.

Bernier had been keeper at Vermilion for 15 years and knew his job very well and at age 46 he was in the prime of his career. He had trained his crew to razor's edge and all were anxious to show their mettle. Back home at the station it may have been a little different. Waiting for the keeper to return was his wife and five young children, one a daughter barely a year old. His wife and the older children might have wondered if they would ever see him again or would he be a sacrifice to trying to live up to an impossible motto? The wives and families of his crew likely thought the same way. The danger the men faced, coupled with the intense desolation of the Shipwreck Coast stations, was sometimes too much to bear!

The Vermilion crew circa 1900. The keeper has changed to James Carpenter. Bernier held the position for twenty years starting in 1880. Author

They reached the beach opposite the *Jones* at 4:00 p.m. Since she wasn't flying any distress signals Bernier and his men made a makeshift camp on the beach and kept a close watch through the long cold night.

The men on the *Jones* likely saw the Life-Savers when they arrived on the beach and must have discussed their situation throughout the night since at daylight on the 30th the U.S. ensign fluttered up mainmast. It was upside down, the tradition signal of distress. Since the range of the line-throwing gun was only 400 yards and the *Jones* was far beyond that, Bernier knew he needed his surfboat to bring the crew off, since the *Jones* was still holding off the bar. He was just picking two men to go back for his surfboat when a messenger arrived telling him Crisp's Point Keeper Robert Small was on his way with his big lifeboat.

After considering Bernier's call for the team, Small doubtlessly concluded a boat would likely be needed. Most of the coast from Grand Marais to Whitefish Point has sandbars running offshore, in many places further out than the range maximum 400-yard range of

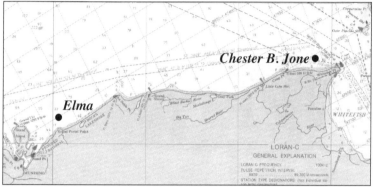

General locations.

the Lyle gun. Thus the only recourse to rescue the crew of the *Jones* was by boat. Keepers and crews backing each other up, as Small was Bernier, were a common feature in the old Life-Saving Service.

Small attempted to launch at his station at 8:00 a.m. but the breakers prevented him from crossing the outer bar and was forced back to the beach. Trying again at 10:30 a.m. he made it across the tumultuous bar. A long hard pull through a gale blown lake lay ahead. Small would likely have spotted the *Jones* around 1:30 p.m. An hour later the Crisp's Point crew slid under the lee of her stern. Captain Nelson of the *Jones* and Keeper Small conferred for a while as to the best course of action. The surfmen also took advantage of the break to grab some rest after their long row from Crisp's. Since Nelson and his crew were certain the schooner-barge would soon be on the bar and totally lost, all seven of the crew, six men and a woman cook, clambered aboard the lifeboat. The lifeboat cast off from the *Jones* at 7:00 p.m. Night was falling rapidly and save for the Vermilion crew's bonfire on the beach, it would be blacker than sin.

Rather than fight through the storm all the way back to the Crisp's Point Station, Small decided to land on the beach opposite the *Jones*. Anticipating what Small was going to do, Bernier had his crew fire up two large torches and a couple of lanterns to illuminate the best site to come ashore. All went well until four or five hundred feet off the beach when the lifeboat capsized in the breakers. Capsizing was something the Life-Savers trained for and it wasn't long before the surfmen soon righted her and got the *Jones* sailors including the woman cook, back aboard. At 8:00 p.m. the big lifeboat propelled by a foaming wave, slid safely ashore. Bernier and his men quickly hitched the team to the boat and hauled her out of the wave's reach.

The *Jones* sailors and Crisp's Point crew were all taken into local dwellings for the night. As it was too late to try to make the long hike back the station, the Vermilion crew spent another cold, miserable night in their improvised beach camp, again watching for the *Jones'* breakup. The gray light of dawn showed her still in position. Her anchors held.

On October 1 the Vermilion crew was finally able to return to the station the next morning noting in the station log, "Well tired out for want of sleep."

As the sea moderated during the night, the following morning Small and his crew launched their boat and returned the crew to the *Jones*. The life-savers also helped pump her out and raise her anchor when the tug *Boynton* arrived to take her to Detroit. Once the tug had the *Jones* safely in hand the Crisp's Point crew rowed back to their station. They too were "well tired out."

The *Commodore* had much less trouble than the *Jones*. Seeing the impossibility of getting another towing hawser aboard from the *Birckhead*, she hauled up her shortened sail rig and made her way down Whitefish Bay. Battered and leaking, she made the Soo a day later.

In spite of the storm the *Birckhead* did manage to pass a towing hawser to the *Elma* and with only one schooner-barge to manage, swung for Grand Island, 80 miles to the west. The seas were rolling high and breaking white but the steamer continued to drag her lone consort westward. They almost made it. Off the stretch of coast called the "Pictured Rocks," the towline broke again. The stress of the storm waves also knocked the rudder off so the *Elma* was unable to even use her minimal sail rig as the *Commodore* did. Truly helpless, she was blown before wind and wave, rolling so badly in the trough of the seas she jumped her masts out. She was soon nothing more than a waterlogged hulk likely barely kept afloat by the lumber jammed in her hold. Deck load long gone, she was drifting rapidly to her death, and that of her crew.

Since the *Birckhead* wasn't able to help the *Elma* and reconnecting a towline was impossible, she left her and ran to shelter behind Grand

Island. The captain hoped the *Elma* would fetch up on the small sand beach near Miner's Castle. It was the only section of shore along the Pictured Rocks that wasn't ship-killing rock.

When she reached Munising the *Birckhead's* captain reported the accident and organized a rescue effort. Since the seas were still running too high to return by boat, he scouted the shore through the woods with East Channel Lightkeeper George Prior. As the men worked their way up the rocky coast they yelled over the edge of the cliffs hoping for a response from an *Elma* survivor. The only reply was the sound of huge waves thundering on the rocks far below. Where was the *Elma*? With the question unanswered they could only return to Munising and wait for the lake to calm when they could use a boat to investigate closer.

Meanwhile things aboard the *Elma* were desperate. Rolling about in the trough opened her seams, flooding her hold, causing the crew to constantly work the old deck pumps to keep her afloat. But the water was gaining. Eventually she went up on a rock reef about 100 feet off Miner's Castle. Captain Thurston immediately dropped his anchors, which pivoted the *Elma* off the reef and eased her pounding. The anchors held all day Sunday but the chains snapped later during the night sending her downwind until she smashed hard on the rock bottom 100 feet from the base of the towering bluffs.

Miner's Castle is about six miles east of Munising. Today it is probably the most photographed feature of the Pictured Rocks National Lakeshore attracting an estimated 300,000 annual visitors.

The colorful sandstone bedrock cliffs between Munising in the west and Grand Marais in the east make up the approximately 17 mile long Pictured Rocks. The cliffs were sculpted into their current shapes by freeze and thaw erosion and glacial Lake Nipissing about 3500 years ago. The layers of sandstone eroded at different rates, creating the sculpted qualities that survive today. The name "Pictured Rocks" was likely given by the old French voyageurs in the 1600s.

In the spring of 2006 one of the two "turrets" of Miner's Castle collapsed altering the distinctive look of the famous landmark. The name Miners Castle is reputed to date from the 1700s when a group of prospectors returning from a scouting trip to the western lake camped at the small river just to the east of the rocks. Since they were miners

The Elma *crew had to scale the high cliffs of the Pictured Rocks to survive their shipwreck. Author*

and saw some eroded minerals in the rocks, they poked around a little but found nothing of value, but the name Miners Castle stuck.

For sailors the area was pure hell. Should a ship be driven into the cliffs or shallow offshore reefs, it was the end of the game. They were nothing but a very long death trap! The rocks were certainly pretty and like a beautifully patterned diamond back rattlesnake - deadly!

The choice to the sailors on the *Elma* was climb or die. Either they managed to somehow scale the rocks to the top of the sandstone cliffs and safety or drown in the thundering lake when their ship finally went to pieces. If they could somehow get a rope to the top then others could use it to make the climb. Finally crewman George M. Johnson of Chicago volunteered to try. He attempted to use the small yawl to row to the base of the cliffs with a line but the waves smashed the boat to pieces against the rocks. Johnson did manage to scramble up the wet and slippery cliff face until reaching safety on a ledge 15-feet long and a bare three feet wide. But he lost the all-important line. It is likely he dropped it while trying to dodge the wreckage from the rudder surging about in the waves at the foot of the cliffs.

Crewman Rudolf Yack of Mount Clemens, Michigan was the next to try. An excellent swimmer he tied a line off to his waist and leaped into the boiling surf, striking boldly out for the beach only to be dashed into the sharp rocks by the waves and killed. When the crew tried to haul him back to the *Elma*, the rope broke and his body drifted off into the lake.

Crewman now attempted to float a line to Johnson by tying the end to various objects. He carefully made his way down from his ledge to the bottom of the cliffs where the surf was smashing, standing by to try to grab a line if it came close enough. He finally managed to snare the line about nightfall but it was too dark to try to bring the crew off so he climbed back to the ledge holding tightly to the end of the hard won rope. Aboard the *Elma* the folks could just hang on through the long and storm striven night and pray for survival.

Once daylight broke Johnson made his end fast to a nearby rock. One at a time the crew used the rope to reach shore, including Captain Thurston's wife and three year old son, the last two making the trip in a improvised bosun's chair. After everyone was off the wreck, the men tied the rope off to their waists and worked their way up the rocks hand over hand, like an Alpine climbing team. They eventually reached a small ledge about 75 feet above the water. After building a smouldering fire they hunkered down to wait for the lake to calm.

The next day at a little past 8:00 a.m., a tug with the lighthouse keeper aboard spotted the cold and hungry survivors. Knowing speed was important, they left Munising at daybreak with the mission of searching the coast for any survivors. When discovered, the *Elma* crew were trying to cobble together a makeshift raft to get back to what was left of the schooner in the hopes of finding some still eatable food in the galley. Rather than make the rescue, the lightkeeper signaled the *Birckhead*, which was about 3 miles out and steaming for the Soo. She promptly came back and picked them up. The steamer had assumed everyone aboard the *Jones* was lost.

Captain Martin Daniels, representing the underwriters, came down from Marquette to examine the wreck. Daniels, a long time member of the city's nautical fraternity, reported the *Elma's* hull was broken and shattered and she was rapidly going to pieces. He was able to salvage only a small part of the lumber cargo stored below deck.

Daniels also reported finding the rope the crew used to climb the cliffs still dangling down the face of the rock commenting "the man who went up there with that line must have been a good one." Daniels and his crew tried to make the same climb and couldn't do it!

The *Elma* was built in 1873 in Marine City, Michigan as a three-masted tow barge. She was a loss of $9,000 and unfortunately carried little insurance. She was 162.5 feet in length, 30 feet in beam and 11 feet in depth.

The tale of the *Birckhead* and her three consorts is typical of what often happened when such vessels were overtaken by strong fall gales and storms. The towing hawser breaks sending the steamer scurrying for shelter and leaving her charges to their individual fates. One uses her marginal and residual ability to sail to reach safety; one survives though barely with her crews removed by heroic action by the Life-Savers and one is totally wrecked, the crew surviving more by sheer will and luck than skill.

References:

Annual Report of the U.S. Life-Saving Service - 1896, pp. 88, 330.

Chicago Inter-Ocean, October 2, 1895.

Cleveland Plain Dealer, September 30, October 1, 1895.

Detroit Evening News, October 1, 2, 9, 1895.

Detroit Free Press, October 2, 1895.

Detroit Tribune, October 2, 1895

Duluth News-Tribune, October 2, 1895.

"List of Life-Saving Station Keepers (Nobel/Raynes)," n.d. RG 26, NARA.

Marquette Mining Journal, October 1, 2, 5, 11, 12, 17, 1895.

Sault Ste. Marie News, October 12, 1895.

✳ 8

PEARL B. CAMPBELL
"A Sudden Burst Of Steam And She Was Gone!"

She was just a tug; plain and work-a-day, grimy and needing a fresh coat of paint and likely a week or two in a shipyard to be put back in prime shape again. But her engine ran reliably and her hull was sound. The 55-foot, 22-ton *Pearl B. Campbell* was built at Saugatuck, Michigan 1883. She did all the normal things a tug was expected to, push and pull the larger ships as needed, move dredges and barges around, tow a raft of logs and sometimes even a little bit of wrecking.

Regardless of her commonplace career, she had her moment of fame, when she sank with all hands in cold Lake Superior on December 7, 1895.

Until she joined the lake's lost fleet there was nothing to mark her as different from the many other tugs earning their daily coal on the "Big Lake."

The end game for the *Campbell* started with the wreck of the steamer *Charles J. Kershaw* in Marquette in September, 1895. (See page 95 for details.) Although the *Kershaw* was completely wrecked her tows, the 206-foot schooner-barge *Moonlight* and 195-foot schooner-barge *Henry A. Kent* were blown on the beach. Fully exposed to the storms of Superior, quick salvage was necessary. The initial salvage job went to Grummond Towing and Wrecking of Detroit. When Grummond failed it was awarded to the Inman Company of Duluth. At the time Captain Byron B. Inman was a major operator of tugs for towing and salvage work. A quick and successful salvage could provide a healthy shot of end-of-year profit.

131

To this end Inman put five tugs to work on the *Moonlight* and *Kent*; the *W.B. Castle*, *Pearl B. Campbell*, *M.D. Carrington*, *Edward Fisk* and *Corona*. All were from his fleet except the *Corona* chartered by Inman from the Osborne Dredge Company. The coal scow *Thompson* was also used. Captain Andrew Rattray was in charge of the operation.

Since both schooner-barges were "on the beach," in effect aground in the shallows between true dry land and deep water, the task at hand was to cut a channel deep enough to pull the vessels into deep water and safety. Digging the channel was easier said than done. Fall storms frequently chased the salvors into the safety of Marquette costing valuable time. Worse, pumps intended to cut out a channel did a fine job with sand but when they hit gravel and clay common to the area, they ground to a halt! To compound the problem the longer the job took, the more sand washed back into the channel so hard won. On December 6, Captain Inman himself came over to Marquette from Duluth to look at the situation. After consulting with his men he pulled the plug on the salvage. The operation cost him $10,000 and since he failed to release the schooner-barges, he wouldn't get a nickel for his efforts. His gamble failed but such is the wrecking business. Both the *Moonlight* and *Kent* would eventually be salvaged but not by Inman.

At the same time he was working to free the two schooner-barges in Marquette he had the tug *J.L. Williams* and lighter barge *J.W. Fee* at Isle Royale working to salvage the cargo of copper ingots from the big steamer *Centurian* aground since October 27. The valuable ingots were jettisoned in an attempt to back the *Centurian* free of a reef.

With the job abandoned, the tugs still in Marquette prepared to run back to Duluth for the winter. All equipment was loaded aboard and lashed down tight. It would likely be a stormy trip and heavy gear rolling about was dangerous to ship and crew.

It was planned the remaining tugs, *Castle*, towing the *Corona*, and *Campbell*, would depart Marquette at 8:00 p.m. on Friday, December 6, but in fact they didn't leave until 1:00 a.m. on Saturday, December 7. The reason for the delay was never fully explained but it certainly isn't beyond the realm of chance the crews took the time for one more short "run" ashore. Having the *Castle* tow the other tugs was a pure economy move. Less coal consumed meant less cost.

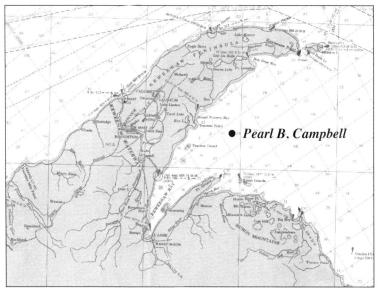

General location.

At first the weather was excellent with the lake flat calm. But the barometer was falling fast as common for December on Superior. Once clear of land the *Castle* headed for Keweenaw Point 60 miles distant. After passing the Keweenaw, it was a straight shot for Duluth of roughly 120 miles including turning the Apostles. The small fleet was running at about eight miles an hour or so.

About 3:00 a.m. the wind shifted north, then northeast and began blowing stiff and hard. To complicate matters a thick snowstorm swirled in reducing visibility to several boat lengths. The fleet continued on to Keweenaw Point, forcing their blunt bows through the building swells. Abreast of Bay de Gris, Captain Rattray gave up the idea of rounding the Point and tried to swing to port and the shelter of the bay but after reasoning that since he couldn't see the bay in the snow turning for it was impossible, he made for Huron Bay 35 miles to the south. Bay de Gris is just under the "hook" of Keweenaw Point and a popular place for ships sheltering from northerly winds.

By this time a tremendous sea was running. When the *Castle* turned, the waves rolled over her bow in a solid mass two feet deep.

She shuttered with their weight and plowed on. Every so often Captain Rattray glanced back and when the snow squalls opened, saw the *Campbell* struggling to keep up but still fast to the tow line. Later men on the *Corona* said the waves ran so high they had trouble seeing the stack from the *Campbell* when she fell into the deep trough. Thick snow squalls continued to come and go, periodically blotting out the world in a swirling white hell.

Captain Rattray also kept an anxious eye on the *Corona* hanging firmly to the long towline. If the line ever broke, a not uncommon event, he could never get another to the tugs under the wild conditions.

The *Castle* had a near disaster when the extreme rolling induced by the turn broke loose one of the big pumps from it's lashing. Crashing free in the hold it threatened to smash open a side. Working with strength and skill born of sheer desperation, the crew managed to secure the pump again, no mean feat given the heaving deck and sliding pump.

Settled on his new course and with the pump secured, Rattray looked back for the *Campbell* but didn't see her. The *Corona* was still there at the end of the towing hawser but behind her where the *Campbell* should be was only empty lake. One of the crew said he saw her just for an instant with her bow pointed high in the air, well clear of the water. He only saw her for a flash, then she was gone to sight. But the captain also clearly heard her whistle. First it was three blasts, then four. Silence followed. Was it a last desperate plea for help?

Rattray thought she fired up her boiler and took her own course through the storm and the whistle signals were alerting him she was leaving. It is likely the captain already had a fire going in the boiler for heat for the crew if nothing else. He therefore could have had steam up for the engine relatively quickly as opposed to a cold start. Keeping his boiler fire going only for heat used a minimal amount of coal opposed to that needed to engage the engine.

The records show confusion at this point. Some maintain the *Castle* ran into Huron Bay for shelter. Others claim they came in behind the Huron Islands. Regardless, by late Saturday the *Castle* and *Corona* were sheltered from the worst of the gale and waited it out. For a while Captain Rattray hoped against hope the *Campbell* would come steaming in out of the snow and drop her hook, too.

———————

The Huron Islands are a group of small islands five miles or so west of the Huron River and near the entrance to Huron Bay. All the islands are described in the *Coast Pilot* as being "bold and deep" except for the most easterly one. Huron Island Lighthouse is located on the most northwestern island. Huron Bay is a dozen miles deep and three miles wide. Considering the geography of the area, it is easy to understand the confusing reports of exactly where the *Castle* and *Corona* sheltered.

The following day when the gale moderated Rattray put into L'Anse and wired Captain Inman of his fears for the *Campbell*. A letter with more complete details was also posted, reaching Inman on Monday. Regardless of Rattray's fears, Inman hoped she was still afloat and had merely sheltered enroute to Duluth. After a week slid by with no word of the tug, it was clear she was lost on the lake with all seven hands; Captain William McGillvray, Mate John Lloyd, Engineer George McCort, second engineer George England, cook Pete McCallin and two unknown firemen. Captain McGillvray and Mate Lloyd were scheduled to be married during their winter lay-up in Duluth. Lloyd was also qualified as a captain but since his tug was already laid up for the winter, he signed on as mate to keep working perhaps with a view to earning some extra cash for his wedding.

It was later claimed the captain's betrothed, 19-year old Catherine McLean of Duluth, had dream in which a man entered her room carrying some ship's papers and a captain's cap. When she awoke the next morning she couldn't shake the eerie dream and then word came of the loss of the tug and husband-to-be.

That the *Campbell* met her end in the midst of the gale was clear to all but specifically how she perished was open to speculation. With Duluth locked tight by winter snow and ice, the fate of the tug was often discussed by marine men. Isolated by the cold and snow there wasn't much else to do in Duluth but talk and the mystery of the *Campbell* was a good topic.

The topic of her loss was revived two years later by marine men when the schooner-barge *Henry A. Kent* foundered in a gale on September 16, in Lake Superior. She was downbound from Ashland, Wisconsin for Lake Erie under tow of the steamer *J.C. Gilchrist* when the seas overwhelmed her near Stannard's Rock. Her crew was rescued with difficulty just before she went dove for the bottom when

———————

the *Gilchrist* pulled alongside in the gale and passed the crew and the captain's two children over on ropes. Later the newspapers charged she was badly overloaded but this is likely just so much hindsight.

During the ensuing newspaper reporting a man claiming to have been aboard the *Corona* when the *Campbell* sank came forward stating he witnessed the disaster. "For a few minutes we had no time to look about us but we could hear her whistle going. Then as we got squared around before the seas we saw her plainly. Her crew were all engaged in trying to clear away the lifeboat from the top of the deckhouse but while we were looking a sudden burst of steam enveloped the *Campbell* and when this drifted away she was gone."

Ominously he also said he knew why the tug sank. Her hatches for the coal chutes were unsecured. Instead the deck side of the chutes was piled with coal. If the tug was running in calm weather, not expecting to take waves over her deck, she commonly left the hatch open with coal piled on it. As the boiler fire was fed from below by the fireman the coal on deck "slid" below down the chute into the bunkers in effect making it self loading. If boarding waves were expected a heavy iron hatch was fitted across the deck chute keeping the engine room watertight. Since the hatch cover wasn't fitted and secured, gale water swept over the decks flooding into the bunkers below eventually drowning the boiler fires.

Assuming the sailor was right, why the *Campbell* failed to secure her coal chute hatch is still unanswered. Was it neglect, Captain McGillvary beguiled by the calm weather when he left Marquette? Or a simple oversight, thinking the hatch was on the chute but hidden by the pile of loose coal above it? When the weather turned foul, why didn't the crew shovel enough of the deck load overboard to secure the hatch? Or was this an impossible task in the screaming gale?

There isn't any doubt the gale was hellacious. The tug *Grayling*, slightly smaller than the *Campbell*, was caught in the same blow. In fact while in Marquette the *Grayling* moored up to the *Campbell* at the dock and the crews became friendly. Before leaving, it was said one of the firemen on the *Campbell* shook hands with his opposite on the *Grayling*, saying they "might never meet again!" Was it a premonition or just a chance remark?

The *Grayling* was running ahead of the *Campbell* when the full fury of the gale smashed into the smaller tug. Her engine room door was stove in by the waves and only heroic action managed to nail planking across the hole keeping the water out. Twice waves swept completely over the diminutive pilot house and forward stanchions broke. Ice formed so thick the captain was trapped in the pilothouse for twelve hours.

The *Campbell* was a loss of approximately $5,000 but the true loss was the seven men aboard her. The wreck of the tug remains missing, hidden in the icy depths off the Huron Islands.

References:

Annual Report, U.S. Life-Saving Service 1896, p. 426.

Daily Mining Journal (Marquette), December 14, 21, 1895.

Department of Commerce, National Oceanic and Atmospheric Administration, National Ocean Survey. *United States Coast Pilot 6*, Washington, D.C., 2002, p. 357.

Duluth News-Tribune, December 16, 1895.

Duluth Evening Herald, October 2, 1897.

Lake Superior Maritime Museum Files: *Pearl B. Campbell*, Inman Tug Line.

Mac Frimodig, *Shipwrecks Off Keweenaw* (Fort Wilkins Natural History Association, n.d.) pp. 21- 25.

Al Miller, "The Loss of the *Pearl B. Campbell*" *Nor'Easter, Journal of the Lake Superior Marine Museums Association*, November-December 1992.

Al Miller, "The Life and Times of B.B. Inman," Nor'Easter, *Journal of the Lake Superior Marine Museum Association*." September-October 1995.

Pearl B. Campbell - Stonehouse Collection.

9

BON VOYAGE

A Most Horrible Tragedy

From the earliest days of sailing wooden ships have been especially vulnerable to fire and extraordinary precautions taken to protect against such a calamity. Galley stoves were bedded in sand and extinguished after every use. Lanterns were never permitted below deck except under very controlled conditions. Since the ships were wood and often heavily layered with very combustible tar as was the rigging for protection against rot, they were sea going tinderboxes waiting for a spark to burst into flames.

With the coming of steamboats many of the old safety prohibitions were modified but fire remained a horrifying ship killer.

Some of the worst disasters on the Great Lakes were due to ship fires. For example, in 1857 the steamer *Montreal* burned in the St. Lawrence River just a few miles from Lake Ontario with a death toll of 250 folks. The *Northen Indiana* went up in flames in 1856 on Lake Erie resulting in the death of 35-56 of the 175 aboard. The burning of the *Seabird* off Waukegan, Illinois in April 1868 took the lives of 102 passengers and crew. The worst of all shipboard fires in American waters was the burning of the paddlewheeler *Sultana* on the Mississippi in 1865 killing over 1,500 Union soldiers. The *Sultana* was transporting mostly wounded veterans back North and the Civil War was over. Evidence now suggests it was arson by a Confederate terrorist (save your Dixie cups, the South will rise again).

It wasn't just the obvious problems of open flame lanterns and careless smoking that torched the ships but sometimes the very engines themselves! Engineers sometimes ran their boilers full blast to gain extra speed. Safety pressure valves were bypassed or disconnected. In the early days of steamboating standards of boiler construction and maintenance as well as licensing of engineers, was at best haphazard. An exploding boiler invariably destroyed the entire ship first by the sheer concussion and second by the resulting fire. In several instances overheated smokestacks caused fires. Engineers had so over fired their boilers the heat was transferred to the stacks, which in turn glowed cherry red! Since the stacks passed through wooden decks and insulation was often nonexistent or very poor, fires resulted. In at least one instance wooden boxes of freight, including cases of matches, were piled next to the smoke stacks! In another example barrels of oil rested against the red-hot stacks.

It is critical for the shipping line and captain, as the owner's on board representative, to maintain shipboard safety equipment, lifeboats that can be successfully launched, life jackets in good condition and fire hoses in working order. Key, of course, is the obligation for a crew to be sufficiently trained to react in an emergency be it fire, collision, storm or otherwise. Sadly the steamer *Bon Voyage* was a disaster waiting to happen. Even in an age of general lack of safety standards, she was a catastrophe unfulfilled.

As Pogo said, "we have met the enemy and he is us!" In the case of the *Bon Voyage*, the owner, captain, crew and owner!

If ever a ship were misnamed, given a name the gods mocked with savage irony, it was the little 150-foot packet steamer *Bon Voyage*. On May 10, 1901 she was bound from Duluth for Portage Lake via Ontonagon when a fire broke out near her stack, evidently caused by the overheated smokestacks. Besides six carloads of general freight she carried 17 passengers and 20 crewmen. She was a fairly new vessel built in Saugatuck, Michigan in 1891. At the time of loss she was owned by the Captain W.H. Singer's White Transportation Company of Duluth and under command of Captain John. P. Foley.

The fire was first noticed about 7:45 p.m. when the steamer was about three miles off shore and heading for the Upper Entry to the Keweenaw Ship Canal.[1] With his ship ablaze the captain tried to beach her but grounded about 75 yards out from the shore and eight long miles from the entrance to the ship canal. Of course, by driving his ship hard to the beach, Foley fanned the flames with his own speed. Since the speed of the ship created airflow running down the length of the vessel, it tended to keep the fire which started in the stack area in the stern away from the bow making the front the only "safe" place to be.

According to published reports, panic reigned supreme aboard the *Bon Voyage*. There was great difficulty launching the lifeboats, getting life jackets and in short, it was everyone for himself. As soon as she ground to a halt passengers and crew alike jumped for it, swimming, paddling, kicking and struggling for the nearby shore while holding onto whatever floated. One desperate woman asked to share a very large plank with a male passenger for a minute while she secured her life jacket but the man holding it refused. Remembering the incident later witnesses said the wood was large enough for at least three people. In extreme situations some men become heroes. Others turn out to be cowards.

An especially poignant tragedy befell four of the five women from the Altman family, the only people aboard lost in the disaster.[2] The group was made up of grandmother, Leah Sharp age 58; mother, Adele Altman age 36 and three children: Bessie, age 15; Annie, age 12 and Mary, age 7. All were Jews en route to a new life in Laurium in the middle of the Keweenaw copper mining district. The husband, Bar Altman, had gone on ahead to prepare the way for his family. Bar had been a small retail businessman in Duluth for ten years but moved to Laurium in April. Finding it a better place for his family he sent for them to join him. The sole survivor of the group was 15-year old Bessie. Her statement is the best record we have of the disaster.[3]

The women were in their cabins in the stern packing their belongings for the imminent arrival when her narrative starts. "Immediately on hearing the cry (of fire), my sisters and I rushed out, meeting our mother rushing to us through the smoke, her face blanched with fear. In less time than it takes to tell it, the upper part of the boat was a bright blaze and not knowing what else to do, we rushed downstairs. There everything was commotion for the whole crew was panic-stricken and nobody knew what to do."

"The hose was turned on but it was in such a condition that only a small amount of water could be turned on the fast spreading flames. Everybody was shouting at everybody else but no body paid any attention to us frightened creatures who where huddled on the lower deck. Around us the men were shouting, above us the boat was on fire and beyond was only darkness, except where the flames bathed the dark, restless waters with an uncanny light.

"When the dining room door opened we rushed in and not knowing what else to do, my mother ran to the cook, begging for help. "All right," said he, and he rushed out locking the door behind him and leaving us with no avenue of escape. The sound of our screams was drowned out by the crackling flames outside and when all hope had failed we discovered a trap door in the cciling which led to the upper deck."

"With great difficulty we squeezed through the opening only to discover that everyone else was gathered on the lower deck on the far end of the boat (author's note - the bow) and that a solid sheet of flame prevented us from reaching that end of the ship at our present level."

"My youngest sister, a child of seven, had wonderfully long, thick braids which reached about to the ground and I can plainly see my mother picking her up, suspending her over the rail and lowering her by those braids to the one man who had responded to our cries for help. I cannot recall one detail about the rest of us descending to the lower deck but we all made it safely except my mother for the next thing I recall is the picture of her floating face upwards in the water."

"The light of the burning boat made her face seem more deathlike and stand out in greater contrast with the dark waters, but her death did not move me in this awful hour... I felt only my duty to save others."

"In order to get to the place where the other people were we had to walk along a foot wide plank which extents around the ship at water's edge, clutching each other's hands as well as the pillars and ropes suspended along the ships side. Each step we took was very difficult and full of danger. We had proceeded only a short distance when I heard a cry and looked around just in time to see my grandmother and younger sister fall into the water. They were immediately lost from view and the last thing I heard of them was the gurgling of water in their throats."

"Now there was only my younger sister and myself left and when I momentarily had to release her hand while stepping around one of the pillars, she too fell into the water. I felt as if I was going to choke... as if my head began to swim and I also fell into the dark water."

"I could feel the water coming through my nose, ears and mouth - if only I could get my head above water and get one good breath! I soon became accustomed to the surroundings and it seemed to me that if it were not for the choking sensations I could be happy."

"It seemed as if I heard the ringing of bells and the singing of children. I could hear my mother's voice say, "Why do you not hurry, Bessie and come to me?" The music was so alluring and I could see my grandmother's face with a smile on it. I knew I was dying and I was wishing it would be soon, for I could join my mother and sisters."

"When I first fell into the water everything seemed so dark to me but gradually it became lighter and lighter - it seemed as if there was a great light somewhere and that I was gradually becoming wrapped into it. Everything about me was beautiful and in the distance I could hear the singing of birds. It was only occasionally that I wanted to breath and then I would think of my father and feel sorry that I should never see him again."

"Suddenly my head knocked against something and I awoke as from a dream, trying to grasp something slippery to which my hands would not cling… it was a log, a beautiful log!"

"Immediately my head was above water. I could breath! I forgot the beautiful sights I had seen, the beautiful things I had heard, my sisters and my mother - I was alive and wanted to live!"

"But what was I to do? I could see the shore off in a distance, I could hear the voices of people, but when I cried for help it seemed that the people on the shore were only laughing at me."

"I do not know how long I floated on the log but suddenly I saw a boat heading in my direction and I cried," Oh please help me: do not leave me behind." They apparently heard me, for soon they were alongside and I was gently lifted aboard the boat. As I reached the deck, I felt an arm about me. The tension was broken and consciousness left me."

It was the men from the tug *Mariel* who pulled Bessie from the water. The *Mariel* was one of three tugs that sped to the scene as soon as the conflagration was spotted.

The lookout at the Portage Life-Saving Service Station saw the fire at 7:50 p.m. and promptly alerted Keeper McCormick of the situation. He in turn quickly got the tug *Fred A. Lee* laying in the ship canal to tow his crew in their lifeboat out to the fire arriving about 8:30 p.m. McCormick discovered the tugs on scene had already recovered two people from the water and the rest had all made it to shore. He searched the water around the wreck looking for more victims without success and finally shuttled 31 of the survivors on the beach out to the waiting tugs. The wet and very cold survivors were taken back to the Life-Saving Station where they were given hot coffee and a warm meal as well as dry clothing from the Women's National Relief box. It was only back at the station the steamer captain told McCormick four of the passengers were missing! Why he waited so long to tell him this vitally important information isn't known. The record isn't entirely clear but apparently the Life-Savers went back out to the wreck to look again for the missing passengers. Considering the very cold water temperature in early May the chances of survival were dim but they had to try. They returned empty handed to the station at 1:00 a.m.

At 10:00 a.m. the next morning a steamer took the survivors to Houghton.

When Bar Altman learned of the disaster he rented a rig (horse and wagon) and drove straight to the Life-Saving Station at the canal entrance arriving around midnight. He discovered his entire family was dead save Bessie and she was, "half dead from fatigue and fright." Her hands and arms were also swollen from holding onto the rough wood fender. The poor girl was taken to a home in Hancock where she slowly recuperated from her terrible physical and mental ordeal.

For the next couple of days surfmen patrolled the beaches and waters looking for the bodies of the Altman women, working long hours in rough weather to accomplish their gristly task. Those of the grandmother and a sister were found the following day on the beach; one discovered just north of the breakwater and easily recovered and the second five miles up the coast. The Life-Savers spotted the second while coasting the shore in their surfboat but the seas were running so high they were unable to land on the rock bound coast and recover it. Instead they returned to the station and hiked overland on a difficult rock-strewn trail to reach it, carrying it seven miles through the woods on a stretcher finally reaching the station at 2:00 a.m. A third body was recovered on the beach on the afternoon of the 12th.

———————

But it wasn't until May 15th the mother's body was found ashore by an agate hunter near the Calumet and Hecla Waterworks. It was a dozen miles from the wreck. As a large piece of wreckage was located nearby, it was conjectured she could have been holding on to it for a long time before finally succumbing. Otherwise it would be hard to explain the distance from the wreck site. The discovery also opens the ugly speculation she may have been alive and hanging on the wreckage for a far longer time than anyone thought. Had the captain told the Life-Savers of the missing passengers while still at the wreck that night could they have found her in time? One paper reported her husband offered a reward of $300 for recovery of the body. Reportedly she had the cash on her person. This may have been pure sensationalism on the part of the newspaper. When the undertaker prepared the body for burial he reputedly found only $60 tucked away in a stocking. Was the $300 stolen from the body by the finder or someone else along the way to the undertakers workshop? Or did the newspaper get the whole story wrong from the beginning?

The funeral of grandmother Leah, and children Annie and Mary was held in Calumet before the recovery of Adele's remains. The three bodies were laid out side by side in simple coffins draped in black cloth. The newspaper claimed the entire population of Calumet was present, a rare event normally occurring only when a mine disaster caused multiple deaths and victims were buried at the same time. All were buried in the small Jewish cemetery near the Tamarack Waterworks.

On October 27, the crewmen of the Ship Canal Life-Saving Service were presented with special gold medals made in the shape of a six-pointed (Star of David) star by the Copper Country Jewish community for their work in recovering the women's bodies. The *Daily Mining Gazette* described them as "elegant gold medals" awarded for their "gallant conduct." McCormick received the largest medal, two inches in length and attached with a clasp. Those for his crew were smaller. Each was inscribed across the top "From the Hebrew of Hancock" and on the bottom with a Hebrew phrase meaning "Thankful for Bravery." McCormick and his crewmen would later receive Gold Life-Saving medals from the Treasury Department for their part in saving the crew of the *L.C. Waldo* in November, 1913, one of the most spectacular rescues in Service history.

Local residents were extremely critical of the *Bon Voyage* disaster, claiming the crew was not familiar with the fire fighting equipment aboard, the davits holding the lifeboats were in poor condition and the life preservers were in bad shape. A coroner's jury examining the death of "Leah Scharf" concurred in this feeling stating, "We the jury find that the deceased, Mrs. Leah Scharf, came to her death on May 10, 1901 by drowning in Lake Superior while a passenger on the burned out steamer *Bon Voyage*. The jury also finds her death is due to the criminal lack of order and discipline necessary in the event of danger on the part of the officers and crew of the said steamer *Bon Voyage*. The jury further find no effort was made by the officers and crew to save the lives of the five women and children passengers. The jury further find no effort was made by the officers and crew at the proper time to launch the lifeboats and that the life preservers were worthless and not kept ready for use in the event of emergency."[4]

Captain Foley was very upset by the ruling, claiming he wasn't told about the inquest and therefore couldn't present his side of the disaster. Virtually all the testimony was against the actions of the captain and crew. The only person speaking for the ship was salesman M. Clos who claimed they acted promptly to avert danger once the fire alarm was given. But his evidence was largely shredded when it was learned he told an opposite story to his friends immediately following the wreck. Even worse, before testifying he supposedly promised Captain Foley he "would not talk too much."

As in the official coroner's proceedings, the truth of what happened on the *Bon Voyage* was well known to the public. On the street there were loud rumblings the crew panicked, that there was no reason anyone should have died, especially not four poor women! Local mariners were vocal in their condemnation of officers and crew.

While this was not an era of heavy government oversight of maritime activity, action was called for and on May 11, the two Federal Steamboat Inspectors from Marquette, Captains Charles Gooding and Charles York, arrived in Houghton to hold an investigation. The formal affair was conducted in the Douglas House Hotel, Captain Gooding asking the questions while Captain York recorded the answers.

The two inspectors tried hard to ferret out the truth of what happened. The hearing started at noon on May 12 and ran until midnight, continuing all day Monday. Following good investigation protocol, they first questioned the lower level officers. The captain would be last.

Engineer James S. Evans said when he learned of the fire he sent his assistant William D. Murphy to investigate. Finding the stack burning, the assistant told the chief to start the pumps (to provide water to the deck fire hoses). He later told the chief, "She's a goner." When she grounded near shore Evans left the engine in slow ahead to keep her fast and came on deck. Running to the gangway with a plank in hand intending to use it for a float, he found a stack of life jackets, apparently unused. He waited until everyone was off the ship but the "colored waiter" who then jumped overboard and swam ashore. Evans said he never saw the captain until he met him standing on the rocky beach. Damnably, he also stated he knew of no fire or boat drills ever being conducted on the *Bon Voyage*.

The assistant engineer testified he found the bonnet around the stack on fire and went to find a hammer and chisel to remove it but by the time he returned, the entire cabin roof was burning and it was too late to do anything. None of the fire hoses appeared to work correctly either. As his chief stated, he knew of no boat of fire drills ever being held and in fact didn't know his assigned station for either emergency! Considering most of the crew were new, referred to by one officer as "green," this is a powerful indictment of the captain's and owner's lack of professional standards.

The problem of fire in the stack wasn't new to the ship. Several of the crew mentioned during the first trip of the season on May 4th the stack area caught fire twice and had to be extinguished by cooling it down with water. No repairs were made to the damage or changes initiated to prevent similar fires. The company simply ignored the problem. The situation is very similar to a chimney fire in a wood burning furnace. The fires can burn very hot and are not uncommonly the cause a numerous house fires.

Mate J. Hawkes told the investigators the captain had him bring the life jackets up from the hold. This was apparently the pile the engineer found by the gangway. The cabins were already burning so he couldn't get the ones from the berths. The lifeboats were also already on fire. He also dropped all the lines he could find over the side to let passengers and crew use them to slide down to the water.

Passengers were adamant the crew only thought of saving themselves. Once the fire started it was "Run for your lives," and "we're off this bucket!"[5] They also complained the life jackets were in bad condition. One of the passengers, traveling salesman W.S. Fain, claimed the crew were panic stricken and refused to even lower a lifeboat. He said the life jackets were in bad condition. He had to use his necktie to tie his on since it had no straps. A couple of railroad men stated the fire hose had been painted over so many times it couldn't be pulled from the holder!

One of the passengers, M. Clos, a cement manufacturer from St. Paul, was a veteran of a ship fire and knew the havoc it created. Above all else he wanted to save the collection of medals his cement won at various fairs and expositions. At the first call of fire he ran to his trunk and removed the medals, pinning them to his coat. When the time came, he leaped into the water and swam to shore, medals and all!

When Captain Foley finally testified, he said the fire started near the smokestack and built so quickly the crew couldn't stop it. Flames prevented his men from even launching a lifeboat but the life jackets were issued to all. He ordered everyone forward but by then the Altman women were trapped in the stern and couldn't be reached. He also claimed he was the last man off the ship and only left after he was certain everyone was in the water. However the chief engineer stated he remained in the engineroom until she grounded, then came on deck. He never saw Captain Foley until he found him standing safely on shore. The captain didn't emerge from the investigation as a hero.

Clearly there were two sides to the story of the fire; the one that young Bessie experienced and was supported by the crew and other passengers, and the one carefully related by Captain Foley. The folks in the Keweenaw were able to see through the "smoke" and knew that when all was said and done, when it really counted, the Altman women were left to die!

The official results of the investigation isn't known, many of the of Steamboat Inspection records are apparently long lost, but Bar Altman did initiate litigation in the U.S. Circuit Court (Western District of

Michigan, Northern Division) against the White Transportation
Company charging the company failed to provide a safe ship, the
officers and men were not competent and neglected their passengers
during the fire, the Altman women were locked in the dining salon and
prevented from getting life jackets and the crew failed to help them.
Certainly the charges were all true. Bar Altman's suit asked for
compensation for the death of his wife, Ada, on the basis of being
deprived of her, "care, comfort, affection, society, counsel and
support," and that she was "skilled in the grocery business and was
capable of earning large sums of money in said business; that the said
Bessie Altman was likewise entitled to the care, culture, nurture, moral
and intellectual training, motherly counsel, advice, instruction,
affection, love and tenderly solicitation..." Bar Altman was also
forced to expend a large sum of money in funeral expenses. He sought
compensation of $20,000, a small enough sum considering his entire
family except for Bessie was wiped out by the steamer fire.[6]

But truth and fairness are not a habitual inhabitant of a courtroom
and the litigation was unsuccessful. The White Transportation
Company managed to have the case transferred to the Fifth Division
of the District of Minnesota in Admiralty under limitation for liability
"pursuant to the several statues and acts of Congress relative
thereto..." This effectively accomplished three things. It fixed the
value of the steamer and cargo based on a surveyor's report; required
all claimants of damage or injury to file their claims on or before
December 17, 1901 and finally limited the liability of the company to
the value of ship and cargo. As a result the suit was settled without cost
to either party. It is worth noting period Admiralty Law also provided
no liability for a fire unless it was caused by "design or neglect" of the
owner. The courts determined the owners exempt from such liability
even though there was "design or neglect" on the part of the owner's
employees or agents. Unless the owner was personally and directly
responsible for the fire, he was off the hook. The only winners were
the lawyers!

The *Bon Voyage* was a total loss of $25,000. All of her superstruc-
ture was gone and the hull burned to the waterline. How much of the
wreck was salvaged isn't known. The following year it was announced
the insurance company sold to Nicolson and Clow, the owners of the

small steamer *Newsboy*. Whitney Brothers of Duluth was awarded the contract. It was felt the machinery and boilers were salvageable but the hull was too far destroyed. While the wrecking outfit was in the area they also planned to work on the *Topeka* in the canal and *Scotia* off Eagle Harbor.

Bessie Altman recovered from her terrible experience and in August 1908 married Louis Kosman in Laurium. The *Calumet News* retold the story of her survival as part of the marriage story but didn't neglect to mention she wore a "gown of white silk, princess style, trimmed with lace." The groom was a typesetter for the local newspaper. Life goes on.

References:

Abstract of Casualty Reports Received, U.S. Life-Saving Service 1876-1914, NARA.

Annual Report of the U.S. Life-Saving Service 1901.

Calumet News, (Calumet, Michigan), August 27, 1908.

Copper Country Evening News (Houghton, Michigan), May 11, 13, 15, 1901; August 19, 23, September 7, 1902.

Harvey C. Beeson, *Beeson's Inland Marine Directory 1901* (Chicago: Harvey C. Beeson, 19010.

Daily Mining Gazette, May 11 - 18, October 2, 27, 1901.

Duluth News Tribune, July 1, 1904.

Robert Morton Hughes, *Handbook of Admiralty Law* - http://books.google.com/books?id=8IgOFUlC2pcC&pg=RA1-PA302&lpg=RA1-PA302&dq=limitation+of+liability+vessel+history&source=web&ots=1V2heUygHU&sig=-nKLT6_qmGJpPuFtLGGDBnbPoKo&hl=en&sa=X&oi=book_result&resnum=1&ct=result#PRA1-PA305,M1, p. 305.

Log of the U.S. Life-Saving Station at Portage, Michigan, May 10-18, 1901, RG 26, NARA.

Marquette Mining Journal, May 11, 18, 25, October 2, 1901.

Sault News Record, May 10, 1901.

U.S. Census 1900, 1910.

U.S. Circuit Court Records, Western District of Michigan, Northern Division, Bar Altman, Administrator of the Est. of Ada Altman, Deceased, Plaintiff versus the White Transportation Company, Defendant. Law Case 480, NARA.

Wells, "History of Accidents on Lake Superior," unpublished manuscript, Stonehouse Collection.

Footnotes:

[1] The timing can be a bit confusing. Many sources say the fire was discovered about 9:00 p.m. I decided to use the times from the U.S. Life-Saving Reports. Part of the timing confusion could be caused by Central versus Eastern time.

[2] The name is also spelled Altmann depending on the source. Likewise some documents will spell Sharp as Scharf.

[3] It is interesting most stories of the disaster refer to the women as "Russian Jews" but only the Grandmother, Leah Sharp, was born in Russia. All the others were born in Duluth. Clearly there was a fair amount of discrimination at work, even as there was great sympathy for the loss.

[4] Some sources will also list her name as Leah Scharf.

[5] My poetic license.

[6] I suspect he only sued for his wife's loss since she had demonstrated economic value to him as an assistant in the store and caregiver to the children. The grandmother and lost children had no economic value, thus, were not part of the litigation. I didn't say the law was fair.

10

MONOHANSETT

A Fiery Death

The port of Alpena was originally laid out in 1840 and was named "Animickee" for the Ojibwe Chief who signed the treaty of 1826, which was negotiated by the famous Indian Agent Henry R. Schoolcraft. The word "Animickee" means thunder, which is why the bay is named Thunder Bay. Schoolcraft was also a geographer, geologist, and ethnologist, noted for his early studies of Native

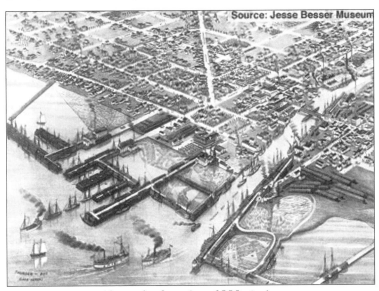

Alpena harbor circa 1880. Author

Fishing boats at Thunder Bay Island, circa 1870. Author

American cultures. He gained access to the tribes through his wife, Jane Johnston Schoolcraft, who was Ojibwe and Irish-American. She shared her knowledge of the Ojibwe language and of Ojibwe legends with him, which became the source material for Longfellow's epic poem, The Song of Hiawatha. The poem, of course, was set on Lake Superior.

Loading wood, circa 1870. Author

Huron Portland Cement, circa 1917. Cement continues to be an important Alpena product. Author

Once upon a time Alpena, Michigan was a thriving shipping center. Vast fleets of schooners carried heavy cargoes of lumber to market and extensive commercial fishing provided considerable local employment.

Today it is just small steel freighters hauling dirty loads of cement from the cement factory and a small fleet of recreational craft forming the bulk of waterborne commerce.

However, the offshore waters abound in shipwrecks, a collection so outstanding in 2000 the federal government established Thunder Bay National Marine Sanctuary and Underwater Preserve, the only freshwater marine sanctuary in the United States, to "manage" the resource. The 448-square mile sanctuary and underwater preserve protects an estimated 116 historically significant shipwrecks ranging from nineteenth century wooden side-wheelers to twentieth century steel-hulled steamers.

One of the wrecks is that of the wooden steamer *Monohansett*. About 10:00 p.m. on November 24, 1907 the steamer was anchored off Thunder Bay Island at the entrance to Thunder Bay when a crewman discovered a fire raging in her engine room. She was upbound to Collingwood, Ontario with 900 tons of coal when northerly gales forced her to shelter behind the island until the lake calmed.

The crewman quickly alerted Captain Joseph Inches of the raging inferno but the fire was too well established and the ship too old and dry for their meager fire fighting gear to have an impact. It wasn't long before the blaze spread forward. But there was sufficient time for most of the crew to save their personal gear except for the engineers living aft although the second engineer John Stockwell singed his hair trying to rescue his kit. The men fled forward to await rescue. The steamer's small yawl was aft and not only too small to carry the entire crew but

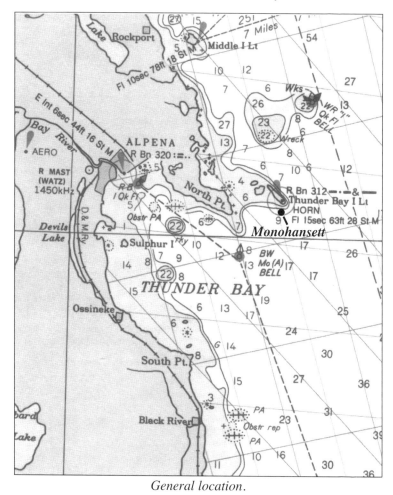

General location.

also a victim of the fire. The local newspaper stated she was "an old boat well seasoned" and "she went rapidly before the blaze and was soon a veritable furnace." It was visible from Alpena, eight miles away.

The second engineer later claimed the fire was caused by a torch tipping over in the engineroom.

Keeper John D. Persons and his Thunder Bay Island Life-Saving Station crew responded promptly to the burning steamer in their lifeboat and safely removed her 12-man crew. The steamer was two miles distant when the station lookout saw the distress signals as well as the billowing smoke. Back at the station Mrs. Persons was prepared with food and blankets for the bedraggled survivors. It was a role she often assumed, succoring the victims of shipwreck.

As soon as Persons returned to the Life-Saving station he notified Captain Peppler of the Alpena tug *Ralph*, which reached the burning steamer about midnight. The tug crew played their two fire hoses on the blaze, managing to finally extinguish it around 9:00 a.m. on Sunday morning. The fire had worked deep into the coal cargo making it far more difficult to snuff out.

In fact the men on the *Ralph* only thought they put the fire out. Late Sunday afternoon it burst out of the coal with renewed fury totally destroying the ship. The drifting hull finally sank about 200 yards off the southwest tip of Thunder Bay Island.

Later that afternoon Persons and his men delivered the steamer crew to Alpena where they took the train for Cleveland.

The 165-foot *Monohansett* was built as the *Ira H. Owen* for the Lake Michigan Transit Company in 1872 by Linn and Craig of Gibraltar, Michigan. She was owned by the Ohio Cooperage Transportation Company at the time of loss.

References:

University of Detroit, Marine Historical Collection - *Ira H. Owen*.

Enrollment Document - *Ira H. Owen*, RG26, NARA.

Herman Runge Collection, Wisconsin Marine Historical Society - *Monohansett*.

Monohansett - Stonehouse Collection.

11

EMMA L. NIELSEN

A Hard Luck Schooner

There isn't any doubt about it. The schooner *Emma L. Nielsen* seemed to be a classic hard luck boat, a "black cat" in the lingo of the old time sailors. Nothing ever really seemed to go her way. Her entire career appeared to be a progression of disasters, large and small, following on each other until ultimately she committed suicide by smashing into a steel steamer. Usually it was the reverse with steel boats cutting down old wooden ships but not for the *Nielsen*.

She began commonly enough, built at Manitowoc during the winter of 1882-83 by Hanson and Scove for local Captain Paul Nielsen. She was named for Nielsen's wife. Many famous sailing ships were built in Manitowoc and their quality was well known. There is no reason to suggest the new *Nielsen* was anything but a very fine schooner. She measured out a bit small, 74.7 feet in length and 62 gross tons, but there was a role for her on the lakes too.

Troubles came early for the *Nielsen*. In the fall of her first year she stranded a quarter mile southwest of the Muskegon, Michigan Life-Saving Station. She was enroute to Ludington with a cargo of hay and flour when she found bottom. Seeing the schooner in distress the Life-Savers launched their surfboat at 3:00 p.m. reaching her only after working their way through a large and very dangerous field of floating logs and other debris. They found the *Nielsen* "completely encased in ice - no part of her but was covered," her three-man crew nearly frozen in her rigging. They were so stiff with ice the Life-Savers had to almost carry them into the surfboat and later from the boat to shore.

Only after warming up next to the cherry-red station stove did the crewmen thaw out sufficiently to tell their tale of shipwreck.

This was the second rescue of the day for the Muskegon Life-Savers. Earlier in the day they recovered the crew of the schooner *Trial* blown against the outer breakwater at the harbor entrance. The keeper later reported the two-man crew, "had been 48 hours exposed to the freezing gale without food or rest and were completely enveloped in ice resembling icebergs rather than shipwrecked sailors."

It seems the *Nielsen* lost her two anchors earlier in the run and when gale winds shifted, was unable to anchor and consequently blew on the sandbar. A week later the when the gales winds dropped off, the Life-Savers assisted a local tug in hauling her off the bar.

She was repaired during the winter but to pay for the work, Captain Nielsen was forced to sell her although he remained as captain. For the next several years she ran wood from the Green Bay area to Chicago.

During the winter of 1889-90 she was lengthened to 98.2 feet to allow her to better compete with larger vessels running the same trade. A third mast was also added. In addition Captain Nielsen managed to obtain two-thirds ownership. The captain was a clever businessman since he also owned a lumber operation just north of Bailey's Harbor on the Door Peninsula that provided the cargoes for his schooner. As time passed the captain focused more on controlling the lumbering side and hired others to "drive" the *Nielsen*.

When the demand for lumber slowed around the turn of the century Captain Nielsen sold the schooner to Lake Huron interests in 1903. Captain David Ferris, one of the new owners, took over as master for the next three years.

During the period Ferris and the *Nielsen* continually managed to find bottom in the area northward of Alpena. In the early morning of June 12, 1904 she stranded on a reef a couple of miles southeast of the Middle Island Life-Saving Station. When the Life-Savers arrived in their surfboat they discovered only her bow was hard on the reef. From midship aft she was "live." The Life-Savers ran an anchor aft then used the windlass to haul up hard and after shifting part of the cargo of posts aft, hauled up hard again until she slid free. A quick look showed she was undamaged and soon was on her way.

On October 20, 1905 she was caught in the same vicious northwest gale that sank the 245-foot four masted-schooner *Minnedosa*, one of the largest sailing ships on the Great Lakes. The *Minnedosa* was torn away from her tow steamer *Westmount* and foundered off Harbor Beach. Eight men and the wife of Captain John Phillips died in the wreck.

The small *Nielsen* tried to shelter from the worst of the screaming winds but she dragged her two anchors until she fetched up on a point 16 miles northwest of Middle Island. The Life-Savers reached the schooner after being towed in their lifeboat to the scene by a tug, then released to make the dangerous run in to the wreck on their own. The Life-Savers tried to take a towing hawser out to the tug in an attempt to haul the *Nielsen* off, but were unable to do so. Working with the schooner's crew they pitched part of the cargo of cedar posts overboard, eventually lightening her enough to come free. A spell in a dry dock followed to put her back in order.

On June 17, 1906 she reportedly stranded at Two Rivers, Wisconsin but after minor effort was hauled free to continue trading. As there is no record of the assistance of the Two-River Life-Saving crew apparently it was a minor and non-threatening incident.

Just over four months later, on October 24, 1906, the *Nielsen* went up on a reef six miles southeast of Middle Island Life-Saving Station. By now "saving" the *Nielsen* was old hat to the Life-Savers. Instead of rowing their surfboat to her, they used the boat's sail rig to make the run. While the Life-Savers regularly trained with the sail rigs for both lifeboat and surfboat, in practice they were rarely used during actual rescues. Again they helped jettison part of her cedar post cargo and she floated free.

Perhaps tired of their "hard luck" schooner in 1908 the owners sold her to another group of three local men. It is interesting that in spite of several changes of ownership her name was never changed. On one hand this was uncommon yet it was also following the old sailing tradition of never changing a ship's "christened" name. To do so was (and among some folks still is) considered bad luck.

For a couple of years the *Nielsen* stayed out of trouble. She didn't find bottom or require the services of Life-Saving crews.

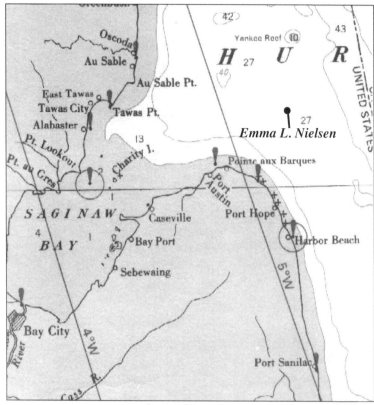

General location.

On June 25, 1911 she was upbound running light from Port Huron at the south end of Lake Huron. Captain A. J. Young, one-third owner of the schooner, was in command. A dense fog hung heavy over the lake. Captain Young was likely on deck listening for fog signals from other vessels but heard nothing.

At 3:00 a.m., June 26, about 11 miles off Point Au Barques, the big steel freighter *Wyandotte* appeared out of the fog and things got very confusing very fast. One version of the tale says the steamer smashed into the portside bow, forward. Downbound with a heavy cargo of limestone the steamer delivered a killing wound, slicing deep into the small wooden schooner. A second version claims it was the *Nielsen* that smashed into the steamer. Regardless of what actually happened the result was the same.

The *Nielsen* was heading for the bottom NOW! The five-man crew had barely time to push her yawl into the water before the schooner dropped out from beneath them. The *Wyandotte* picked up the men and continued on to Port Huron as if nothing had happened and as far as she was concerned, nothing did since the only evidence of the accident was some scratched paint forward.

The *Nielsen* remained hidden in Huron's depths until 1980 when shipwreck hunters Larry Coplin and Dave Trotter discovered her. Trotter reported, "The *Nielsen* lies with a slight list to her port side and is virtually intact except for the damaged bow section."

References:

Annual Report U.S. Life-SavingService 1884, pp. 160-161; *1904*, p. 168; *1906*, p. 97; *1907*, p. 109.

Emma L. Nielsen - www.boatnerd.com.

Walter M. and Mary K. Hirthe, "The *Emma L. Nielsen*" *Wisconsin Marine Historical Society Soundings*, Volume 23, Number 3, 1983, pp. 1-5.

"*Emma L. Nielsen*," *Anchor News, Manitowoc Maritime Museum*, November-December 1983, p. 144.

Times Herald (Port Huron, Michigan), October 18, 1987.

David Trotter, "The *Nielsen* EXPERIENCE," *Diving Times*, April-May 1982, pp. 1-3.

12

ROUSE SIMMONS

A Sordid Tale

This is a story of greed pure and simple! But intertwined throughout is human drama, innocent victims caught in the deadly web of "easy" money. And there is also the history of Great Lakes sail overarching the entire sorry affair.

I realize I am taking a far different tack than nearly every other writer who has scribbled on the infamous *Rouse Simmons* affair. Likely I will offend some of them as well as readers too used to the sanitized versions of this sordid tale. I expect to take their broadsides double-shotted and shrapnel too! As the old captain would say, "I'll have none of that bilge water! Batten the hatches and padlock the halyards! I ain't stop'n this old wind wagon for devil himself!"

Today unfortunately the entire "Christmas Tree Ship" mess is viewed through very rose-colored glasses with the result that an event that should have been a moralistic tale on greed has assumed the mantel of redemption, the struggle of mere mortals against the malevolent power of storm whipped Lake Michigan. But let's start at the beginning of this grimy tale.

The schooner *Rouse Simmons* was built in Milwaukee by Allen, McClelland and Company in 1868. At 123 feet long, 28 feet in beam and 8 feet in depth, she was a fair sized vessel for the times. She was a bit unusual in that she had two centerboards instead of the more common one. Retractable centerboards were an important feature on Great Lakes sailing craft as they could be raised when moving in shallow rivers and harbors but lowered for greater stability and

165

Two Christmas Tree schooners at a Chicago Dock. Author

improved sailing characteristics on the open lake. She had a long career largely befit of notoriety and controversy, just a work-a-day ship doing her job.

The newspaper report of her construction and launching was very complimentary. "...the *Simmons* combines speed with speed with large carrying capacity and in this respect must be considered faultless. Her entrance, although seemingly full, is nevertheless quite sharp and her run is really beautiful. The timber used in her construction is the finest we have ever seen put into a vessel and the manner in which it has been put together reflects the highest credit upon the builders. The cost of the new vessel when completed and ready for sea will be in the neighborhood of $17,000. She will carry three masts, fore and aft rigged with a square sail on the foremast. Her owners are Royal B. Tousley and Captain Akerman of Kenosha, the latter of whom will have command. The *Simmons* is designed for the lumber trade and will ply between Manistee and Chicago."[1] The last sentence is very revealing as it potentially places her in the middle of the illicit lumber trade. See the chapter on the *Alvin Clark* for more details of this most fascinating part of Great Lakes history.

She was named for the Kenosha industrialist who helped finance her. He was part of the Simmons family that later founded the Simmons Company most famous for manufacturing mattresses.

Other than as a general description of the *Rouse Simmons* I wouldn't place too much value in the previous news item relating to construction. In 40 years of maritime research I have never found a launching account describing the ship as a pig made of the worst possible timber, poorly finished and sure to be lost on her first trip!

Most of her working life was spent trading for Charles H. Hackley, a lumber baron based in Muskegon, Michigan. Season after season she hauled timber from the mills to market in the growing cities of the Great Lakes. When the great forests were largely cut off, the schooner became just excess inventory and Hackley sold her.

Her working career was marked by a normal number of accidents, major and minor. Bumping into docks and every so often a bridge as tugs hauled her through narrow rivers were commonplace as was damage in storm and gale. The ultimate accident happened when she sank in Traverse Bay. Salvors pumped her out and after a cursory refit she was back in business.

As common to all of the old wind wagons, the *Rouse Simmons* never carried a lifeboat. The best they had was a small yawl usually hung from davits across the stern. It was used as a general workboat around the ship and to occasionally land crew if the ship anchored out. Often they didn't even have a set of oars. A single oar was sufficient to scull her about so why have more?

She gained her eventual passage into Great Lakes legend as the "Christmas Tree Ship." According to the popular story Chicago folks looked forward to buying their evergreens (trees, wreaths and garland) from the schooner tied up in the Chicago River at the foot of the Clark Street Bridge. A huge banner hung from her masts proclaiming, "The Christmas Tree Ship - My Prices Are the Lowest," and a dangling string of electric lights helped draw the customers to the ship. The deck was covered with thousands of trees and city dwellers flocked to buy their special tree from the "special" ship. It was a marketing device worthy of Sam Walton!

This version of the Christmas Tree Ship concept was a sales gimmick developed by two brothers, August and Herman Schuenemann. Eventually wives and daughters were involved in the business also. For roughly forty years, from 1887 into the 1930s a Schuenemann Christmas Tree Ship was in Chicago selling trees, etc. Instead of going to the shopping center parking lot to buy a tree as we do today, folks just went to the ship and hauled one off for a cost of 75 cents to a dollar. It became a tradition for many Chicagoans to make the trip to the river at Clark Street to buy their special Christmas Tree.

The trees were carried down on the ship from the great pine forests of northern Wisconsin or the Lake Michigan shore of the Upper Peninsula of Michigan. Both areas were long logged out of marketable timber but the cut over forests were perfect for small fir, aka Christmas Trees.

The Christmas Tree schooner trade was inherently dangerous for several reasons.

First the trees had to arrive reasonably fresh, which mean shipping in late November, always a stormy time on Lake Michigan. There is a reason why most traffic was off the Lake by this time. The danger to ship and crew outweighed the financial gain.

To maximize profit, the ship had to carry as many trees as possible. Trees were stuffed tightly into the hold and piled high on deck. Overloading and stability of the ship were not taken as issues of great importance.

Transportation cost had to be minimal. Modern freighters were too expensive for low value retail Christmas Trees. The only cost effective option was to use old sailing ships. The wind was, after all, free and the old sailing ships nearly so!

And it was the last factor, old sailing ships that made the trade so dangerous and fully exposed the inherent greed of the owners.

By 1912 commercial sail on the Great Lakes was nearly extinct. Where once great clouds of canvas covered the Lakes, now seeing an old windjammer was an oddity to be remarked upon. There were many reasons why sailing ships disappeared and all involved efficiency and safety in some aspect.

There is an old saying that "a boat is a hole in the water surrounded by wood, steel, iron or more recently fiberglass into which the owner

Captain Herman Schueneman. Author

pours large amounts of money." While usually taken to refer only to recreational boats, in fact it is valid for all watercraft, large or small. Maintenance is a continuous requirement. A ship not used regularly is one in the process of slow (or rapid) deterioration.

The old sailing vessels were notorious maintenance hogs. From the day wood for the hulls was cut in the forest it began the inexorable process of deterioration. Framed wooden hulls continued to worsen needing work and plank replacement on a regular basis for example to remain seaworthy. Using the wrong or unseasoned wood in construction or replacement accelerated the deterioration process. Canvas sails, running and standing rigging were equally hungry consumers of maintenance money. A failure of any of the three areas could and often did, spell disaster as surely as a navigational error. A ship owner sending a ship to sea in anything but a fully maintained condition is signing a potential death warrant for his crew. The evidence shows when Herman took the old *Rouse Simmons* north for trees he signed not only his own warrant but also his crew's. The reader can judge the value of my arguments.

Both August and Herman Schuenemann were first generation German Americans arriving in Chicago in 1884. The city had a massive German community in 1904, equaling roughly ten per cent of the city's two million population, so the two brothers fit right in to the community. To put it all in perspective, at the time there were twice as many Germans as Irish in Chicago.

The first disaster to the brothers occurred in 1898 to the small 75-foot schooner *S. Thal*. The schooner was 31 years old, ancient for a schooner, and only 53 gross tons. She was purchased the month before for a mere $200, a number reflective of her elderly and decrepit condition. Just as bad, August had to borrow money from a Sturgeon Bay merchant to buy his trees! If you can't even pay for a low price cargo of cut over trees, certainly there isn't any money left to actually maintain the ship. The whole operation was run on a thinnest of shoestrings! That August would willingly risk his own life was one thing but to callously jeopardize those of his two crewmen was deplorable.

After loading an estimated 3,500 trees and hundreds of bundles of greens at Jacksonport, Wisconsin she headed for Chicago.[2] On November 9 she was overtaken by a strong gale off Glencoe, Illinois. She was only a short distance from Chicago when the blasts caught her but it might as well have been a thousand miles. She dropped her anchor in a hopeless effort to ride out the gale but she was a flat-bottomed beast and certainly not fit for facing a gale on the open lake overloaded with Christmas Trees. It was another instance of needlessly putting lives at dire risk for slimmest of personal gain.

Her battle with the gale was seen from shore by the daughter of the manager of the Chicago Associated Press agency. She quickly alerted her father to the drama unfolding before her eyes. He in turn notified the U.S. Life-Saving Service Station at Evanston on the campus of Northwestern University. Reportedly, the seas were running too high for the Life-Saving crew to attempt to reach her in their surfboat and she was too far offshore for the breeches buoy. It was one of the few instances the Life-Savers were helpless to act.

Several Chicago reporters dashed north on the train to see the tragedy playing out on the stormy lake. One of them, Alexis J. Coleman, a *Chicago Times-Herald* writer, later provided a description of the wreck featured in the 1935 *Chicagoan*. "We learned that in the afternoon while men were watching the ship, then about a mile and a half from shore, both sails had been set in a lull, she had been headed northeast into the wind, anchored to ride out the gale; that a heavy gust had torn the foresail to shreds, the vessel tossed, spun around the foremast snapped a few feet above deck and that men had been seen clearing away the other mast; that what looked like a curtain or spread had been raised as a distress signal on what remained of the foremast. We learned that quantities of young evergreen trees were being washed ashore, with a miscellany of broken timbers. Doubtless a sand-bar prevented the ship from getting closer to shore."

The Windy City scribes carefully climbed down the steep bluff to the beach below finding it covered with flotsam from the schooner. Broken timber and Christmas Trees were everywhere. "Chests, doors, pieces of rail, broken timbers showing rot where bolts had gone through;" it was silent evidence of the utter destruction of the *Thal* and her entire crew. The reporters duly returned to Chicago and wrote heart-wrenching stories of the death of the "Christmas Tree Ship." It was so much romantic claptrap. The *Thal* was grossly unsafe, well "used up" and poorly maintained, overloaded and sailing at a time of year that was at best foolhardy.

Regardless of the loss of the *Thal* and his brother August, Herman resolved to carry on the enterprise. After all, business was business! Perhaps the loss of the *Thal* was even an advantage, providing a heavy dose of sympathy to the surviving brother's tree sales.

Herman used a variety of sailing ships to make the annual tree runs, including the *Ida, Truman Moss, George L. Wrenn, Jessie Phillips, Maggie Dall, Mystic* and *Mary Cullins*.[3] Reportedly he wrecked the last schooner in a late season gale also but managed to save himself. The story goes that he was bound in to Thompson, Michigan on the south shore of Michigan's Upper Peninsula late in the year. On the dark and stormy night he spied a light ashore and mistook it for the expected one at the end of the village dock. Instead it was a lantern in the second floor of a log cabin a half-mile east of the harbor! As the result of his error the schooner drove high and dry on the unforgiving limestone shore. She was a total loss. He also wrecked the *Mystic* near Little Bay de Noque west of Thompson in 1895 and he had to charter the schooner *M. Capron* to bring the already cut trees to Chicago. His profit that year was minimal, putting added pressure on the next season.

Herman was different from many of his contemporaries in that he didn't wholesale trees to retailers. He only sold retail, cutting the middleman out of the business and maximizing his own profit. Establishing the deck of a schooner, aka the "Christmas Tree Ship" as his point of sale was a vital part of his business plan. There was nothing noble about what he did. It was just good business.

In 1910 Herman purchased a one-eighth interest in the *Rouse Simmons*. Captain Charles C. Nelson of Chicago had an eighth and Mannes J. Bonner of Beaver Island had the remaining six-eighths share.

By 1912 the *Rouse Simmons* was 44 years old, ancient for a Great Lakes schooner, even if she had first class maintenance all those long years. Instead she was in desperately bad shape. Regardless of her condition, Herman had a business to run and that meant bringing trees to Chicago so off he went with her to Michigan's Upper Peninsula and the small village of Thompson, for the last 20 years his favorite shipping point. In 1910 he started the Northern Michigan Evergreen Company with an address of the Northwest corner, Clark Street Bridge. By 1912 he owned 240 acres of cut over land near Thompson. Clearly he was expanding his operation. The Thompson locals liked his annual arrivals since it meant extra money for them cutting and hauling the trees. The great stands of White Pine were long gone and the local men had scant opportunity to earn ready cash. Perhaps even better the young pine trees were becoming a cash second growth from the old cut over land.

In the ensuing days the crew stuffed the schooner with trees. They were usually packaged in bales for ease of stowage. One source claims it was 35,000 trees and another only 5,000 but the exact number is immaterial. She carried as many as she possibly could find room for... anywhere. Every tree was green money to Herman.

Herman also loaded an especially tall tree as a gift for a leading theater in Chicago. In return for his gift, the theater provided a season's box for his family and friends.

To maximize the number of trees he could carry he constructed a second deck on the schooner. Built with 1 inch x 12 inch x 16 foot hemlock boards it rose about 10 to 11 feet off the actual deck. While it provided more cargo room it also affected her center of gravity increasing the danger of capsizing and provided more area for wind to "grab."

There was another use for the makeshift deck too. When he reached Chicago he installed stoves and sewing machines in it and used it as a work area for a gang of local women to make up evergreen wreaths, etc. Customers could watch them being made, adding to the sales allure.

———————

This is a very revealing photo of the Rouse Simmons. *Note how deeply laden she is with an apparent load of trees stacked on her deck. She does not appear to have the temporary second deck as carried on her last rip. Rutherford Hayes Presidential Library*

The effect of the temporary deck and the huge piles of trees was to raise the mast booms far above their normal position. Special crutches were built to allow them to rest ten feet or more above their regular saddles. This also meant taking reefs in the sails to compensate for altered set decreasing vessel speed and to some degree maneuvering. The temporary deck and tree load also restricted access to her hatches, bilge pumps and pin rails making working the ship far more difficult.

The schooner was so covered in trees she looked like floating green haystack to one observer. In fact she was far closer to a floating pile of trees than a sailing ship.

How many people were aboard the *Rouse Simmons* when she plunged to the bottom of Lake Michigan is an open question with the number ranging from ten to 17 depending on the source. In some instances their identity is also an open issue. Without a doubt Herman Schuenemann was aboard as was Captain Charles Nelson. Apparently

The Rouse Simmons *evidently without cargo. Note her high freeboard. Her wheel was behind the small aft cabin. K.E. Thro*

Herman was present in the role of cargo owner while Nelson filled the job of Captain. Steve E. Nelson was the mate, sailors Charles Nelson (not the captain), Frank Carlson, Engwald Newhouse (aka Ingvald Nyhouse), cook Albert Curta (also identified as Albert Lykstad) and woodcutter Philipp Bausewein are reliably placed aboard. The rest of the folks are more illusive. Some sources assert sailors Philip Larson and Gilbert Swanson were aboard as were lumber shovers William Oberg, Seven Inglehart, Jacob Johnson, Jack Pitt and Andrew Danielson. Others say Captain Nelson's wife was also aboard. Depending on the sources used, the following are also credited with going down with the schooner: Mate Alex Johnson and sailors Edward Minogue, Frank Sobata, George Watson, Ray Davis, Conrad Griffin, George Quinn, Edward Murphy, John Morwauski, "Stump" Morris, Greely Peterson, Frank Faul, Jacob (John) Johnson and Edward

Hogan. Different published lists also confuse the jobs of sailor, tree cutter and lumber shover so telling who did what is more perplexing. Adding more mystery to who was actually aboard, about six months after the wreck a trunk came ashore with "*Rouse Simmons* - J. E. Lathop" stenciled across it. None of the various crew lists I found contain any mention of a Lathop.

The whole issue of who was aboard is complicated by the claim some lumberjacks from Thompson hopped aboard the schooner for a cheap ride down to Chicago for the holidays. They never appeared on a manifest and likely no one ever cared whether they lived or died. The same could be true for some of the crew. If they left no caring family behind, who really gave a hoot whether they were aboard or not? Although this may seem overly callous, they were only sailors, lumberjacks and roustabouts, not people most folks took any real notice of dead or alive. It can be a cruel world.

Historian Frederick Neuschel estimates Herman had roughly $3,000 invested in the trip, a substantial sum for 1912. Money was needed to pay the sailors and tree cutters, feed them all, towing fees to get the schooner out of the Chicago River, into and out of the harbor at Thompson and back into Chicago. The wind may be free, but tugs weren't and their captains demanded payment. Canadian historian C.H.J. Snider considered each trip essentially a, "go for broke" venture. Failure meant economic disaster. Conversely, when Herman returned with a full cargo and enough time to sell them, his investment could be doubled or tripled. Restated, Herman was operating on the economic edge. Wasting money on schooner maintenance was not part of the business plan. On the way back to Chicago in 1911 she reputedly was leaking so bad he had to stop and recaulk her. Whether the work was properly done in an actual shipyard or just a temporary fix in a quiet cove isn't known. Given his financial situation it is more likely he simply careened her as best he could in a calm bay and had the crew pound in rope strands in the worst of the opened seams. Snider also claims Herman was being sued by a merchant over an old debt and he was forced to sell half of his tree land to satisfy it. Under this type of economic stress money to caulk the schooner in a shipyard just wasn't available. Unfortunately caulking was vital to a wooden ship, especially the old schooners when their hulls "worked" in a seaway. Caulking wasn't a do it yourself project. The ship had to be drydocked, the old caulk torn out and new pounded in. It was an important skill peculiar to specialized yard workers.

The schooner hauled out of Thompson on November 22. Weather conditions were not good. A stiff breeze was blowing and it gave every indication of building into a northwest gale but Christmas Trees didn't sell in Thompson. The market was in Chicago and every day spent in port was a wasted day for selling the trees.

One old-timer from Thompson reputedly related that a friend of his who was a retired lake captain had a remarkably accurate barometer. When he saw the precipitously low reading he told Herman not sail but send the trees down by rail instead. Herman refused, saying "he wouldn't miss the trip for anything."

There is a story that as the schooner left Thompson a tug passed inbound with another schooner seeking shelter from the building gale. The tug's captain supposedly said, "that crazy Dutchman's going out in this... with every inch of canvas up!"[4] Another tale claims the captain of the schooner *Butcher Boy* commented, "I wouldn't go out in this blow for all the trees in the woods. Those boys will be lucky if they even see Christmas."

Yet another observer noticed she was riding very low in the water, so low her outer bobstays were submerged![5]

Under normal conditions the trip could take three or four days. But conditions were not good and by the 28th she was only off Kewaunee, Wisconsin, barely half way to Chicago. She was one of the few vessels still on the lake. Most had run for shelter when the first blasts of wind howled over the water.

Why the *Rouse Simmons* didn't head for shelter is an unanswered question. The obvious response is Herman didn't think he had to! Just keep on going and the gale will blow it self out. There is also the problem of sailing a haystack of Christmas trees. She was likely barely controllable so neatly tacking into a safe harbor was well neigh impossible. Because she was so loaded with trees and had a makeshift second deck added so she could carry even more trees, the crew's ability to trim or adjust her sails necessary for a course change was minimal and given the icing conditions, likely impossible. In short, once she cleared Thompson she was committed to Chicago come full

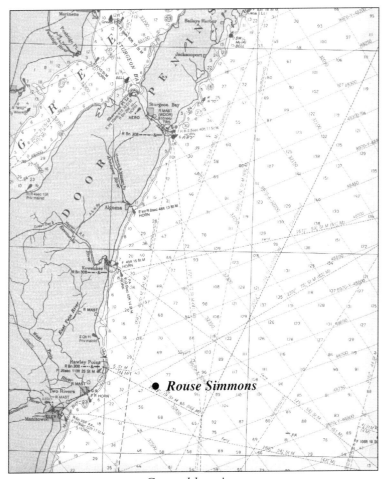

General location.

gale or flat calm. For those aboard it was literally a case of life or death. There wasn't any middle ground.

Several folks on shore claimed they saw her flying distress signals and in obvious trouble.[6] Gale winds were screaming at 60 miles an hour and the old schooner must have been taking tremendous punishment. After she was posted missing the steamer *George W. Orr* reported sighting her in distress to the Revenue Cutter *Tuscarora*, which in turn searched the location in question for her but found nothing. The *Orr's* crew said the *Rouse Simmons* had faded off into the low scudding clouds and disappeared. Or was it even worse?

About 2:50 p.m. the lookout at the Kewaunee Life-Saving Station, Number 6 Surfman S.J. Loft, reported sighting a schooner about five or six miles out with a flag at half-mast. Keeper Nelson Craile climbed up to the tower and used the marine glasses to confirm Loft's report. He saw the unknown schooner was flying a distress signal and already was off to the East Southeast and rapidly drawing

Captain George Sogge led his crew in a forlorn effort to find the Rouse Simmons. *Author*

away under short sail. Considering the poor visibility in the strong northwest gale it was surprising Loft spotted her at all.

In the howling gale Craile knew his ability to help was dependent on finding a tug to either tow his boat out to the schooner or go out alone and tow her into safe harbor. Kewaunee hadn't received any of the new motorized boats and there was no chance his crew could catch up with her in a rowing boat. If a tug could get him close to the schooner, maximum effort by his crew at the oars should enable them to lay up to her and rescue the crew. But he needed a tug to get him close. The only tug in the harbor that could do the job was the *Industry*. When he went get her he found out she had left much earlier for Sturgeon Bay 20 miles to the north. Without a tug Craile and his men had no chance of reaching the schooner.

Once he was certain he was powerless to help Craile telephoned Keeper George E. Sogge at the next station to the south at Two Rivers

The U.S. Life-Saving Service Station at Two Rivers, Wisconsin.
Wisconsin Maritime Collection

at 3:10 p.m. alerting him to the schooner's plight and that she was heading his way.

Two Rivers Life-Saving Station had a motorized lifeboat, an innovation that greatly increased the range and capability of Life-Saving crews. The developmental work on motorized boats was started in Marquette on Lake Superior in 1899. Under the leadership of legendary keeper Henry Cleary the Marquette station crew worked with a local engine manufacturer, Lakeshore Engine Works, to test the value of the new engines for the Service. The tests were successful and as funding allowed, the Life-Savers modified their surfboats and lifeboats to a new motorized configuration.

The Two Rivers crew lost little time. Within ten minutes of Craile's call, "Captain" George E. Sogge and five of his men launched their 34-foot motor lifeboat and headed out to intercept the schooner. There were eight men assigned to the station. One was on leave and one was left on watch in the tower leaving six surfmen to crew the lifeboat. The Service lifeboat was one of the finest coastal rescue boats ever developed. They were built to be virtually unsinkable, to keep going into the worst of gale and storm. There wasn't any hesitation among the Two Rivers crew and doubtlessly remembering the Service's motto, "Regulations say we have to go out, they say nothing about coming back," Sogge and his men did their duty. But it was horribly miserable out on the wild lake and the surfmen were suffering badly. The seas were running high and cold, freezing on the deck of the little lifeboat and covering the oilskin clad Life-Saving Services surfmen in ice.

Sogge later related, "I immediately launched my power lifeboat and at 4:20 was rounding the Two Rivers Point six miles north of the station. I then expected to see the schooner. We could see nearly to Kewaunee but there was nothing to be seen. I kept on running north about eight miles from the point; then changed my heading out in the lake for one hour. By this time it was dark. There was nothing to be seen of the schooner, nor wreckage nor signals. It started to snow heavy and considering we had been making a very thorough search for the distressed vessel and that I had done all in my power and all there was in my judgment to do in the case, we set our course for the station. The trip, as might be imagined, wasn't a pleasant one, but our only regrets were that we had put forth our best efforts in that direction without avail."[7] They found nothing and at 8:00 p.m. returned to the station. It was a long and difficult run with naught to show for it.

Later surfmen patrolled the beach looking for survivors but came up empty-handed.

Captain Craile and the Kewaunee Life-Savers came under some criticism for not rescuing the crew from the *Rouse Simmons* when they spotted her in distress. It was rumored the Schuenemann daughters were upset as would be understandable. The *Sturgeon Bay Advocate* also printed a mud-slinging letter castigating the Kewaunee crew for not responding. By condemning the Life-Savers the writer only exposed his own ignorance of the circumstances surrounding the disaster and the real limitations of off shore rescues in oar powered boats in a roaring gale. Since the writer only identified himself as "G.C.", he protected his own lack of knowledge from public ridicule.

Some mariners thought it was impossible for the *Rouse Simmons* to sink. She was a wood ship jammed full of trees. How could she sink? They claimed she was likely dismasted and just drifting around

The Ann Arbor 5. *Could she have rescued the crew of the* Rouse Simmons? *Author*

on the lake somewhere. There were examples of lumber schooners refusing to sink due to the timber jammed into the holds providing tremendous buoyancy.

Reportedly the big steel carferry *Ann Arbor No. 5* spotted her three miles north of Kewaunee and roughly five miles offshore. The watch reported the schooner's mainsail was down but she was flying a staysail, jib and reefed foresail, laboring heavily and heeled hard over. The ferry captain approached to within a half mile and took a good look at her but since he saw no distress signals he continued on his way to Sturgeon Bay for shelter. Given this very creditable observation Herman must have put up distress signals after the *Ann Arbor No. 5* passed and before coming within visual range of the Kewaunee Life-Saving Station lookout.

There is of course another explanation. The *Rouse Simmons* was flying distress signals and the *Ann Arbor No. 5* chose to ignore them! Perhaps the captain felt any attempt to rescue the crew would place his own ship in danger so it was best if he just looked the other way and left her in God's hands. Later he was accused of doing exactly that and vehemently denied the charge. It is a question that will never be answered.

When built in 1910 the 360-foot *Ann Arbor No. 5* was the largest carferry on the Great Lakes. She was a well found and capable vessel built to batter the worst of Lake Michigan.

Certainly the *Rouse Simmons* was overwhelmed by the gale rather than suffer loss by other marine hazard such as collision or running aground. It can be hypothesized her huge deck load of trees could have acted as sponges, soaking up the water and attracting ice adding more and more weight to the schooner not only affecting her ability to rise to the seas but also stability. The question became did she simply dive for the bottom or take a knockdown, then plummet into the depths like a leaf spiraling down from a tree?

For a while marine men thought the *Rouse Simmons* had taken shelter somewhere and would soon show up. Sailing vessels were notorious for turning up all right days after a storm. It wasn't to be. By the end of November wreckage washed ashore on the Wisconsin shore near Two Rivers and Kenosha. Unless there was a name on it, determining what ship it came from is very difficult. But the evergreens told a different story. Thousands of trees arrived on the beaches, not only on the Wisconsin shore but across the lake at Pentwater, Michigan, too. One old-timer stated the lake was green with trees. Area commercial fishermen also found their gill nets heavy with them. For years afterwards small numbers continued to find shore, as it they were being released from the wreck in dribs and drabs as a constant reminder of the disaster.

Herman's daughters, minding the store in Chicago, kept up their hopes long after others accepted the bitter truth. The schooner *Minerva* came into the Chicago River ten days late and *George Marsh* and *Mossack* arrived covered in thick ice. Surely their father would make it too! He always did before.

Some marine men held out optimism the *Rouse Simmons* survived the gale for an inordinate period. Newspapers around Lake Michigan printed stories of ships reported lost showing up days later. If they could do it, why not the *Rouse Simmons*? A number of erroneous sighting reports fueled the desperate hope of the Schuenemann women, but hope isn't reality and gradually it became obvious to even the most diehard optimist the schooner and her crew were gone forever, victims of the Lake Michigan gale.

It isn't hard to imagine the last hours of the *Rouse Simmons*. Herman evidently tried to run her under the lee of the Wisconsin shore as long as he could. But overloaded with trees and consequently carrying little canvas, sailing terribly, she was driven by the wind without being able to keep a course. As the gale grew in intensity conditions on the old schooner grew more and more dangerous and soon she was pitching and rolling horribly, each movement straining her ancient timbers and ill-maintained rigging. Freezing spray soaked into the deck load trees making them heavier and heavier further increasing her top heavy condition. The massive amount of trees on the deck and ill-advised second deck made access to her rigging and sails very difficult, further eroding the ability to control her.

When seas began to wash aboard the lashings holding the trees in place loosened and soon trees were going overboard singly and in bundles. Any attempt by the crew to secure them would have been hopeless. Likely crewmen could have been washed overboard while either trying to relash the trees or swept away by an especially powerful boarding sea. Given the dreadful gale there was no chance of anyone rescuing the men even if their situation was noticed! The schooner was uncontrollable and the yawl hanging from the stern davits (if it was even still there and not yet knocked off by the waves) wasn't capable of being launched or surviving under such horrific conditions.

Waterlogged and unmanageable, the *Rouse Simmons'* only hope was to somehow stay afloat long enough to either blow ashore or be rescued by a Life-Saving Service crew. Both were very big <u>Ifs</u>. Going ashore in such a gale would likely destroy the ship and crew with it. If the Life-Savers even spotted her through the flying scud and snow, whether their surfboat could survive the crashing waves was debatable. At least Herman knew the Life-Savers would try.

The men aboard the *Rouse Simmons* likely tied themselves off to a mast or other substantial part of the schooner, hung on and prayed. The more hopeful may have still worked the huge hand bilge pump trying to drive as much water out of her as they could but the deck load affected their access to the pump. Whether the pump worked or not is also debatable. A vessel poorly maintained is no guarantee equipment will work, especially when most needed.

The Schuenemann women were made of tough material and made the best of the disaster. When Herman's wife, Barbara, realized she was now the sole provider for the family, including her young daughters, Elsie, and twins Pearl and Hazel, she went right to work mere days after the disaster. After obtaining the use of the schooner *Oneida* from a friend, she salvaged some of the trees from the *Rouse Simmons* and brought others down from the Upper Peninsula by train and continued the family business. Luckily Herman had contracted for the rail delivered trees before leaving Thompson. With the *Oneida's* deck filled with trees, business went on as usual. Barbara even put up a new sign, "Captain and Mrs. Schuenmann's Daughters," in an effort to play on the shopper's emotions. Christmas is a season of emotion and she would use it to the family advantage. Regardless of her efforts a post Christmas report in the *Chicago Record-Herald* indicated it was a disastrous season and the family was facing bankruptcy. Money was still owed to the tree-cutters in the Upper Peninsula as well as other business obligations. The paper estimated indebtedness of $8,000, a small fortune in 1912.

Many of Herman's friends offered to help the family but since virtually all of Schuenmann money was invested in the tree cargo, the loss was extreme and numerous lean years were ahead. A special relief fund was also established by the Chicago maritime community to provide for the families of the men lost aboard the schooner. How much was ever raised and how it was disbursed is unknown but it certainly never compensated for the loss of a loved one.

For several years after the loss, Barbara went north to Thompson to buy trees and ship them south by rail. In later years she used both ships and rail as circumstances dictated. She reportedly quit when she realized it was man's work and people were taking advantage of her. Apparently 1925 was the last year she sold trees from the deck of a schooner in the river.

No shipwreck story is complete without a note in a bottle telling of the last desperate moments and the *Rouse Simmons* is no exception. Some were thought false while others had the ring of truth.

In mid December, 1912 fisherman Michael Kovlovik discovered a bottle floating off Sheboygan and out of curiosity ran his boat up to it and recovered it. It was sealed with a wood stopper evidently whittled from a fir tree. Inside was a penciled note: "Friday, Everybody goodbye. I guess we are all through. Seas washed over our deck load Thursday. During the night the small boat was washed over. Ingvald and Steve fell overboard Thursday. God help us. Herman Schuenemann." The note is commonly considered a hoax by many folks but the Schuenemann family apparently considered it genuine.

On April 23, 1913 the Captain's wallet was discovered at Two Rivers Point by lightkeeper Henry Gattier. It seems Captain Norman Allie of the local fishing steamer *Reindeer* came in with a pile of nets to dry. As is common, the nets were filled with weed picked up from the lake bottom. The weed was unceremoniously dumped on the ground and the nets strung up on the large wood reels to dry. The light keeper was apparently jawing with Allie and idly kicking at some of the weeds when he accidentally discovered the wallet. The area the nets were set was thought by many to be the spot the *Rouse Simmons* sank. The wallet was wrapped in an oilskin cloth and sealed with a large rubber band. The contents could still be read but gave no clues to the last moments of the ship.

Just days later Captain Manville LaFond of the Two Rivers fish tug *Monitor* reported hauling up a human skull in his nets set in the same area. He said it was the third skull he recovered. What happened to the gruesome relics is unknown. The same fisherman reported he earlier hauled a skeleton up but it spilled out of the net before he could drag it into his boat. Everyone assumed these were remains from the *Rouse Simmons* crew.

Other than the bones, the lake reportedly never gave up a single body of anyone aboard the schooner! At least none were ever positively identified as from the wreck (with the exception of an incident yet to follow). All remained captured forever by Lake Michigan.

On July 31, 1919 the *Sturgeon Bay Advocate* carried a story about a young boy finding a message in a bottle on the beach seven miles north of the ship canal. The boy was helping his father and uncle tend a pound net when he discovered the bottle buried in the sand. He was getting ready to toss it back into the water when his father stopped him, noticing a piece of paper was rolled up inside. Breaking the bottle open revealed the message: "Nov. 23, 1912, these lines were written at

Rouse Simmons *under all sail. Note her high free board. Author*

10:30 p.m. Schooner *Rouse Simmons* ready to go down about 20 miles southwest of Two Rivers Point between 15 and 20 miles offshore. All hands lashed to one line. Goodbye. Captain Charley Nelson." Like the earlier note, opinions vary concerning authenticity.[8]

In the end whether any of the notes were authentic or just pranks is pure speculation. Although Schuenemann family members thought the first was genuine sometimes the power of wanting something to be true can overwhelm what is true. We sometimes believe what we want to believe.

The Schuenemann's continued to sell Christmas trees until 1933 when Herman's wife Barbara died.

Daughters Pearl and Elsie sold trees for a while with the help of an old sailor named "Big Bill" Sullivan. He claimed to be the sole "survivor" of the *Rouse Simmons*, maintaining he went north with the schooner and helped cut and load trees but didn't like the weather and turned down the "free" trip back to Chicago, taking the train instead. Over the years his story became more embellished and although there was no record of a "Sullivan" on the crew list, he <u>was</u> good for business and that was what counted.

Another sailor claimed he refused to sail in her because her ballast stones were removed to allow her to carry more cargo. Without heavy ballast her ability to stay upright was severely affected. Even a common sailor knew that!

There is a story too about a lumberjack named Hogan Hogensen who was going to take the schooner back to Chicago until he thought better of it. He supposedly saw her rats leaving her on the mooring lines while she was still in Chicago but went up with her to Thompson anyway. Perhaps surrounded by the loneliness and stark oppression of the dismal north woods he decided to take the hint and ride the train back to the city. Doubtless too he remembered the old sailor's superstition about rats deserting a sinking ship. If the rats said, "Get off this old bucket," he would take their advice. He was later said to have been killed in a saloon brawl in the city.

There are other tales of premonitions too. It was said an ominous feeling pervaded the dock at Thompson before the schooner left. Crew and landsmen all felt something was wrong, something hanging out in the gray lake and dark clouds that wasn't good.

The *Chicago Record-Herald* reported Captain Nelson's daughter said her father told her he had a premonition something would go wrong on the trip. She begged him not to go but he said he had told Herman he would and couldn't go back on his word.

Given the inability to nail down the actual number of men aboard the schooner, there is also the rumor she carried 13 folks. Some of the Chicago papers enjoyed playing up this angle.

The *Rouse Simmons* left Thompson on a Friday too. One of the oldest sailing superstitions revolves around Friday. No ship's business should be conducted on a Friday, or launching, or any significant activity. And above all, never start a trip on a Friday. If necessary, delay until one minute past midnight but leaving on a Friday only guarantees bad luck.

There are also tales of phantom bells ringing about the time the *Rouse Simmons* perished. Supposedly vessels around the lake heard

188 * WOOD ON THE BOTTOM

ship's bells ringing when there were no other ships around. Some folks believed phantom bells rang when a ship somewhere on the Lakes sinks.

And you can't have phantom bells without a phantom ship or two. Since the *Rouse Simmons* is now officially part of Great Lakes legend sailors claim to occasionally see her still booming south off Kewaunee, trying evermore to deliver her cargo of Christmas joy. It is claimed the best times for sighting the ghost ship are either on the anniversary of her loss, Christmas Eve or Christmas Day, or so go the tales!

The wreck was discovered on October 30, 1971 by Milwaukee scuba diver G. Kent. The schooner was resting upright in approximately 180-feet of water, roughly nine miles off Two Rivers and remarkably intact given the circumstances of loss. The name was still evident and her hold still held Christmas trees. One of the great mysteries of Lake Michigan was solved.

The masts are down and deck badly torn up and covered with debris as would be expected. The anchor windlass is still on the bow. Her stern and bow are unbroken. Considering her depth, she is a fairly frequent target of divers.

Since this was well before the imposition of state rules governing recovering objects over time many articles were lifted from the wreck including her anchor and miscellaneous small artifacts. Some including a name board are on display at the Rogers Street Fishing Village and Museum in Two Rivers. The anchor is on display at the Milwaukee Yacht Club and additional items have been on view at the South Shore Yacht Club. Reputedly, a single skeleton (or parts there-of) was found under timber in the stern area and it was reverently buried in the sand near the schooner.

While the wreck was in remarkably good condition it was strange her steering wheel and related gearing mechanism required to control the rudder is missing. What happened to it? The wheel itself missing is one thing but the entire mechanism is unheard of!

Part of the mystery was solved in 1999 when a fish tug hauled the wheel and attached mechanism up in her nets about a mile and a half north of the wreck. It was a heavy lift since the steel wheel and mechanism weighted approximately 400 pounds. Clearly it didn't just fall off the *Rouse Simmons* but if it was lost during the gale there was no way to control the ship and she was doomed.

How the wheel came to be off the ship was the big question. At first a theory was based on the bundles of trees on deck freezing into solid blocks of ice, breaking loose and smashing into the wheel mechanism eventually breaking it off, sending it overboard. In the end this theory was discarded as unlikely considering the damage to the wheel and strong bolting holding the mechanism to the deck.

A close look at the wheel shows several spokes beat back at 90-degree angles. Others were missing completely. Something either struck those spokes very, very hard or applied great force. The prevailing theory is that the mizzen boom broke loose and smashed into the wheel knocking it out of its deck fastening and sending the whole shebang overboard.

The mizzen boom is a very heavy spar the foot of the mizzen sail was laced to. It was designed to swing port and starboard (pivoting on the mast) as needed to control the ship. Heavy tackle at the outward end of the boom called a mizzen sheet should secure it in place and controls its port to starboard action. The foremast and mainmast also had similar booms. Should the boom break loose of her controlling rigging and driven by a wide enough swing, it could hit the wheel with great force. Given repetitive strikes it <u>could</u> have driven it clear of the deck mounting and given the correct circumstances of rail damage and circumstances it <u>could</u> have knocked it overboard.

This is of course only a theory and there are a number of significant points working against it.

The mizzen throat halyard and mizzen topping lift <u>should</u> have helped control the elevation of the boom. If the boom started to swing wildly the motion <u>should</u> have been well above the wheel, thus not striking it. In addition the mizzen sheet at the head of the boom <u>should</u> have kept it under tight control. I know of no other shipwreck, fresh or saltwater, where a runaway boom smashed the wheel and send it overboard. That said, there always is a first time for everything.

For the boom to break loose the mizzen halyard, mizzen topping lift and mizzen sheet would have had to all catastrophically fail. This would be a direct and damning evidence of an appalling lack of maintenance of the *Rouse Simmons*.

Under normal circumstances if the boom did break free, it is possible the sailors could have captured it with rope and made it fast.

It would have been extremely difficult to do so in a gale, however, not impossible on a normal schooner. But working on the floating haystack the *Rouse Simmons* was transformed into by Herman's foolishness in loading every possible tree he could would have vastly added to the difficulty and perhaps made it utterly impossible.

The Kewaunee Life-Savers reported she only had the fore sail and jib top set, implying the main and mizzen sails were lowered and secured. The booms would also have been secured. This was common and accepted sailing practice. Considering the gale, running under fore and jib wasn't unreasonable. Keeping the main and mizzen sails down (furled) was necessary to prevent her from taking a knock down from the wind blasts. This means the mizzen boom should have been secured in her crutch and therefore locked from movement. Breaking loose from this position would have been extremely difficult. The crutch was a stanchion from the deck with its upper end formed to receive the boom thus securing it from unexpected movement.

The 10 to 11-foot high deckhouse Herman added to allow the ship to carry more trees would have changed the dynamics of the boom lifting it that distance above it's normal position. Considering the boom in it's usual position would have cleared the wheel by at least three feet, it was now a good 13-feet above the wheel. Even if the boom broke free of the mizzen sheet it's swinging arc would have been a dozen feet above the wheel thus could not have hit it.

Since the stern of the *Rouse Simmons* is still intact and shows no evidence of the boom smashing a wheel and mechanism through it, this theory is further degraded. Portions of the wood wheel box supports also appear relatively undamaged. If the boom was smashing into the wheel there should be some evidence of it on the box.

Based on the above reasoning, my belief is the wheel and related mechanism was not knocked off the schooner by the boom striking it. I think it more likely it was yanked off the ship much later by a net from a commercial fishing tug. The net fouled on the wreck and in the act of being hauled free broke the wheel and mechanism from the schooner damaging the spokes. The mechanism in turn slipped from the net dropping in the location where it was dragged up the second tug. While this is certainly very speculative, I think it more probable than the boom theory. But again it is an opinion and readers are fully capable of reaching their own conclusions.

If the missing wheel is discarded as the direct cause of loss, then what happened? My guess is because the ship was generally unmanageable due to overloading and second deck, she was unable to either seek shelter or respond adequately to gale damage. Tremendous amounts of water entered her through the poorly caulked hull and her pumps were either unable to keep up with it, or the second deck and outlandish load of trees prevented the crew from using the pumps. She sank lower and lower in the water becoming more and more vulnerable to the seas. Boarding waves swept across her deck sending "unattached" men overboard. Eventually she either took a knockdown or just dropped to the bottom.

Herman's Christmas tree business wasn't unique but it was the last operation of any significance. The tree business started around 1876 and at one time 50 or so small schooners would lay-up in the Calumet basin with trees for sale. The schooners were small enough to work into the little ports not served by larger vessels or railroads. North Woods merchants were eager to provide a quick load of trees for cash or barter and the captains just as eager to bring them down to the big city for a quick end of season influx of cash. If they didn't sell every last tree they could always be used for firewood. The Charlie Noble always had to be fed and unsold trees worked just fine.[9] Something good would come of the gamble. In the early days sailing ships were (generally) well-maintained working vessels. It was only at the end of the sailing ship era they truly became death traps.

The Christmas tree fleet didn't last long since the very nature of the trade was based on the availability of many small schooners. As the Great Lakes fleet grew up, moving into steam, iron and steel, the small schooners were squeezed out of the game. Without the small schooners to transport the trees cheaply and the availability of captains willing to gamble on both hauling the trees and selling them, the entire business collapsed. Herman Schuenmann was soon the last captain in the trade and he was living on borrowed time.

Christmas trees were always a very bulky cargo with little per item weight as opposed to a bulk cargo of iron ore, for example, which provided far better stability. A vessel packed with a hold full of

The Rouse Simmons *at her Chicago dock with a load of trees.*
Author

thousands of trees and thousands more stacked ten foot high or more on the open deck was comparatively light and also very tender. Without the stabilization of a weight in the hold (as ballast), she was prone to blow over in a sudden gust of wind let alone survive a real gale. Running tree-laden schooners to market was, therefore, always a very chancy deal. Once loaded, the captains hoped for a spell of light northerly winds and that the wind would hold long enough to make her intended destination. In the fall of the year on the Lakes this was often an unlikely proposition.

Herman's credentials to master a schooner were as good as anyone else's. There were no "maritime schools" or governmental accreditations for sailing captains. The training was hands on and very inconsistent. Typically, after several years as a common sailor, a man with the right attributes stepped up to mate and after a few more years of experience, captain. Or if he had the money or credit, just buy a ship and become an instant captain. For example, Herman's brother August started his career by buying a share in the schooner *W.H. Hinsdale* from John R. Doak, a local captain. Previously, August worked as a sailor for Doak. Before August turned 30 he was a captain.

It was a far different time than the highly structured training and evaluation process of today. The "good old days" weren't always so good.

The turn of the century was not a good time to own a sailing ship on the Great Lakes. The maritime industry was rapidly shifting from sail to steam and good paying cargos were few and far between for the old wind wagons. Many of the schooners had their rigs cut down and became mere barges towed obediently along behind smoke belching steamers. A couple men rode them to handle the simple tasks of handling hawsers as needed. Sometimes, one of the hands was a former sailing captain who could find no other work. So much for the glories of sail!

Without the schooner to provide a viable living, owners like August and Herman were forced to do what they could to keep bread on the table. For a time they worked the retail grocery trade, then it was coal, later wood and hay. They even ran a saloon for a while. Some businesses were more successful than others but regardless, every Christmas season they went north for trees. If things worked out right the trees would provide enough income for the year or cover losses in other enterprises. They were always living close to the economic edge.

Oft times the schooners were not by any stretch of the imagination seaworthy. For example, Captain Clark, a contemporary to the Schuenmanns in the tree business hauled the schooner *Kate Hinchman* out of a marine graveyard the week before he sailed her north for trees. She was sunk deep into the mud bottom with only her gun whales awash when he pumped her out and pressed her into service. For want of a frowning storm god it could have been the *Kate Hinchman* as the "Christmas Tree Ship".

Following the loss of the *Rouse Simmons* a short item appeared in a Chicago newspaper claiming a local sailor related the schooner was "...full of soft planks and in bad condition. If heavily laden when she met a hard blow probably every seam opened."[10] While any after the fact allegation should always be viewed somewhat skeptically, this one has the stolid ring of truth.

When the *Rouse Simmons* was finally decreed lost with all hands the Chicago newspapers had a decision to make. Did they treat the story as a normal shipwreck, just another in a long list of lake disasters, or expose the economic corruption leading the loss of ship and crew? Instead they chose a third option, wrapping the loss in the mantle of the "Legend of the Christmas Tree Ship" and her noble captain. They in effect "created" the news and built the Christmas Tree Ship legend into one that still sails blithely through the imagination today.

The "facts" of the Schuenmanns and the *Rouse Simmons* passed into Great Lakes legend and were shamelessly "spun" by flocks of so called journalists. What started as a businessman sending rotten schooners into November gales so he could capitalize on seasonal Christmas tree sales became some sort of "Captain Santa Claus" providing trees for all out of the goodness of his heart! If he tried the same scheme today the ship would be prevented from sailing for its decrepit condition and he may well be enjoying Christmas behind bars for reckless endangerment.

This nonsense has gone so far the Coast Guard has been convinced to revive the "tradition" by using a cutter to deliver a symbolic load of trees to Chicago every December. That the Coast Guard, charged with enforcing maritime safety, is in effect celebrating one of the worst offenders, is indeed black comedy.

There are folks who will argue the "legend" of the Christmas Tree Ship is really driven by romantic notions of the great age of sail. Wreathed in the mantle of wooden ships and iron men Herman became a living Santa Claus and the *Rouse Simmons* a seagoing version of his sleigh. The crew must be the reindeer. As I said before, this is so much claptrap and utterly devalues human life, even if they are "only" sailors.

It is impossible to excuse unscrupulous captains and owners sending rotten, poorly maintained and overloaded ships to sea in a desperate chase for profit. That they were able to find crews willing to sail these death ships speaks volumes to the decline of sailing opportunities on the Lakes. It was either crew aboard a hulk like the

Rouse Simmons or don't crew at all and for men with no other skill than sailing, this was no real choice!

There are also folks who will retort times were tough for the Schuenemans and making the annual Christmas tree run was their only real chance for economic survival. This may be so, but it surely is no reason to place innocent crewmen at dire risk.

A third argument holds ships and sailors were expendable during this period of history. The loss of a ship and crew was unfortunate but really not unexpected. In the end the *Rouse Simmons* was just an unfortunate accident. This is more claptrap and no excuse for an owner sending a rotten ship to sea, especially overloaded with cargo.

It can be argued that Herman wasn't really responsible for the loss of the *Rouse Simmons* and her crew. He was only the owner of the cargo and one-eighth of the ship. Captain Nelson was the actual captain of record and therefore responsible for all decisions relating to the safety of ship and crew. As they say in Tennessee, "That dog don't hunt." Herman was the man in charge of the whole operation, boat, trees and crew. Sixty-eight year old Captain Nelson only agreed to come out of retirement for the trip to help out his old friend, 41-year old Herman. It was Herman who ordered her out into the gale. Nelson, a veteran of 50 years sailing on the Lakes, should certainly have known better than to tempt the storm gods.

And so ends the real *Rouse Simmons* story, nothing more than a greedy captain and a rotten ship overwhelmed by a Lake Michigan gale, at least in my opinion.[11]

References:

Ann Arbor No. 5 - http://www.michiganshipwrecks.org/annarbor5.htm.

Mary Blahnik, "The Story of the Christmas Tree Ship," *Shipwreck Journal, the Journal of the Great Lakes Shipwreck Historical Society*, Winter 1996-97, pp. 6-9.

Dwight Boyer, *Lore of the Lakes*, (Freshwater Press: Cleveland, 1940), pp. 170-171.

Theodore Charrney, "The *Rouse Simmons* and the Port of Chicago," *Inland Seas*, (Winter 1987), pp. 242-46.

Chicago American, November - December 1912.

Chicago Inter-Ocean, November-December 1912.

Chicago Record-Herald, November-December 1912.

Chicago Tribune, November - December 1912.

Howard Chappelle, *The History of American Sailing Ships* (W.W. Norton: New York, 1935), pp. 268-272.

"Christmas Tree Ship," *Grand Marais Pilot and Pictured Rocks Review*, nd, p. 4-B.

Harry Hansen, *The Chicago* (Rinehart and Company: New York, 1942), pp. 239-245.

Fred Hollister, "Loss of the Christmas Tree Schooner," *Sea Classics*, January 1977, pp. 6-11, 82.

Journal of the U.S. Life-Saving Station at Kewaunee, Wisconsin, November 26-30, 1912, RG 26, NARA.

Journal of the U.S. Life-Saving Station at Sturgeon Bay, Wisconsin, November 26-30, 1912, RG 26, NARA.

Journal of the U.S. Life-Saving Station at Two Rivers, Wisconsin, November 26-30, 1912. RG 26, NARA.

Roger LeLievre, "A Christmas Tree Tale," *Michigan History*, November-December 1981, pp. 26-27.

Frederick Neuschel, "Bringing Christmas Trees to the City," *Chicago History Magazine*, December 1992.

Neuschel, *Lives and Legends of the Christmas Tree Ships* (Ann Arbor: The University of Michigan Press, 2007), pp. 14, 15, 144, 158, 169, 174, 183, 185, 202,203.

Manistee Pioneer-Tribune, October 12, December 20, 1978; April 17, 1924.

Milwaukee Journal, January 4, 1961; November 27, 1974; December 5, 1971; December 24, 1973; November 22, 1975; November 20, 1987.

Milwaukee Sentinel, November - December 1912, August 15,

September 4, 1868; March 23, 1977; November 26, 1981.

Rochelle Pennington, *The Historic Christmas Tree Ship, A True Story of Faith, Hope and Love*, (Pathways Press, 2004) pp, 63-64, 105, 111, 118-120, 166, 217, 233.

Roger Pilon, *Harlow's Wooden Man*, "Christmas Tree Ship," Winter 1978, pp. 6-7.

William Ratigan, *Great Lakes Shipwrecks and Survivals*, (Galahad Books: New York, 1960), pp. 38-39.

PA3 Paul Roszkowski, USCG, "Renewing a Chicago Tradition," *Great Lakes Cruiser*, February 2001, pp. 44-46.

Rouse Simmons - www.boatnerd.com.

Rouse Simmons - Stonehouse Collection.

Rouse Simmons - Runge Collection, Wisconsin Maritime Historical Society.

Sturgeon Bay Advocate (Sturgeon Bay, Wisconsin), November - December 1912, July 31, 1913.

Sheboygan Press. November 22, 1975.

C.H.J. Snider, "Christmas Tree Ship," *Toronto Telegram*, December 22, 29, 1945.

The Tale of the Christmas Tree Ship - *http://images.google.com/imgres?imgurl=http://www.wisconsinhistory.org/highlights/archives/simmons2*.

Wisconsin Weekend Magazine, December 11, 1974, pp. 3, 8.

Footnotes:

[1] *Milwaukee Sentinel*, August 15, 1868.

[2] The reported number of trees loaded is questionable but the overloading wasn't .

[3] AKA "COLLINS"

[4] There are several variation of this tale. Some attribute it to the tug captain, others to the schooner captain. All are common in expressing shock that Schuenemann would start for Chicago when the weather was plain bad and clearly going to become far worse.

⁵ A bobstay is a hold down for the bowsprit. Running with her bobstays so low meant she had very little freeboard and was in an overloaded condition.

⁶ Some of these reports were doubtless hindsight.

⁷ *Sturgeon Bay Advocate*, December 26, 1912.

⁸ A second version of the note reads: "These lines were written at 10:30 p.m. Schooner R.S. Ready to go down about 20 miles southeast of Two Rivers Point between 15 and 20 miles offshore. All hands lashed to one line. Goodbye. Nelson." It was assumed Nelson was Captain Charles Nelson but it could have been the mate Steve Nelson. Note the inconsistency of 20 miles southeast versus southwest.

⁹ A British merchant captain, Charles Noble, is said to be responsible for the origin, about 1850, of this nickname for the galley smokestack. It was said that Captain Noble, discovering that the stack of his ship's galley was made of copper, ordered that it be kept bright. The ship's crew then started referring to the stack as the "Charley Noble." Over time it became a generic term for a wood burning ship's stove.

¹⁰ *Chicago American*, December 4, 1912.

¹¹ It is worth noting that Herman could have shipped the trees by rail and continued to sell from the deck of an old sailing ship thus maintaining the gimmick of the "Christmas Tree Ship" but not needlessly endangering the lives of his crew. But the old schooner provided cheaper transportation regardless to the danger to his crew.

ABOUT THE AUTHOR

Frederick Stonehouse holds a Master of Arts Degree in History from Northern Michigan University, Marquette, Michigan, and has authored many books on Great Lakes maritime history. He is the 2006 recipient of the Association for Great Lakes Maritime History Award for Historic Interpretation and received the 2007 Marine Historical Society of Detroit Historian of the Year Award. *Steel On The Bottom, Great Lakes Shipwrecks, Great Lakes Crime, Murder, Mayhem, Booze & Broads, Lake Superior's "Shipwreck Coast," Dangerous Coast: Pictured Rocks Shipwrecks, The Wreck Of The Edmund Fitzgerald, Great Lakes Lighthouse Tales, Women And The Lakes, Untold Great Lakes Maritime Tales, Women And The Lakes II, More Untold Great Lakes Maritime Tales, Final Passage, True Shipwreck Adventures, My Summer At The Lighthouse, A Boy's Journal* and *Cooking Lighthouse Style, Favorite Recipes From Coast To Coast* are all published by Avery Color Studios, Inc.

He has also been a consultant for both the U.S. National Park Service and Parks Canada, and an "on air" expert for National Geographic Explorer and the History Channel as well as many regional media productions. He has taught

Great Lakes Maritime History at Northern Michigan University and is an active consultant for numerous Great Lakes oriented projects and programs. Check www.frederickstonehouse.com for more details.

His articles have been published in numerous publications including *Skin Diver, Great Lakes Cruiser Magazine* and *Lake Superior Magazine*. He is a member of the Board of Directors of the Marquette Maritime Museum and a member of the Board of Directors of the United States Life Saving Service Heritage Association.

Stonehouse resides in Marquette, Michigan.